NUTCA

LAND LAW

AUSTRALIA
LBC Information Services
Sydney

CANADA and USA
Carswell
Toronto · Ontario

NEW ZEALAND
Brooker's
Auckland

SINGAPORE and MALAYSIA
Thomson Information (S.E. Asia)
Singapore

NUTCASES

LAND LAW

FIRST EDITION

by

CHRIS CHANG
LLB, Barrister (U.K.),
Advocate and Solicitor (Malaysia)
Senior Lecturer, LLB Programme Leader
School of Law, Middlesex University

JOHN WELDON
LLB, LLM Dip. A & S Law
Principal Lecturer
School of Law, Middlesex University

London · Hong Kong · Dublin
Sweet & Maxwell
1997

Published in 1997 by
Sweet & Maxwell Limited
of 100 Avenue Road, London, NW3 3PF
http://www.smlawpub.co.uk

Reprinted 1998

Phototypeset by J&L Composition Ltd, Filey, North Yorkshire
Printed in England by Clays Ltd, St Ives plc

No natural forests were destroyed to make this product:
only farmed timber was used and re-planted

ISBN 0 421 597100

**A CIP catalogue record for this book is available
from the British Library**

CONTENTS

TABLE OF CASES

TABLE OF STATUTES

1. THE MEANING OF LAND

The Definition of Land

Introduction

The *Law of Property Act 1925* section 205(1)(ix) defines land as including land of any tenure, and mines and minerals, whether or not held apart from the surface, buildings or parts of buildings (whether the division is horizontal, vertical or made in any other way) and other corporeal hereditaments; also a manor, an advowson, and a rent and other incorporeal hereditaments, and an easement, right, privilege or benefit in, over, or derived from land; but not an undivided share in land.

Apart from the soil, ground or earth, the word land includes the buildings on the land, fixtures attached to the land, mines and minerals and incorporeal hereditaments (such as easements and profits a prendre). The Latin maxim, *cuius est solum eius est usque ad coelum et ad inferos*, which means, that an owner of the land owns everything from the depths of the earth up to the heavens, describes generally, the extent of the ownership of land. In reality, the exceptions to this maxim means that this maxim is, as described by Griffiths J. in *Bernstein of Leigh (Baron) v. Sykviews & General Ltd* [1978] Q.B. 479 (see below), nothing more than "a colourful phrase".

Fixtures and Chattels

KEY PRINCIPLE: *The ownership of land includes ownership of fixtures on the land. Section 62 of the* Law of Property Act 1925 *further provides that a conveyance of land is deemed to include inter alia fixtures unless otherwise provided.*

Holland v. Hodgson 1872

The question arose as to whether spinning looms which were attached to the stone floors of the rooms in a mill formed part of the land.

HELD: That the spinning looms were to be regarded as fixtures and were therefore part of the land. (1872) LR 7 CP 328.

COMMENTARY

Blackburn J. suggested that the degree of annexation and object (or purpose) of annexation were the important criteria for deciding whether an item is a fixture or not. Subsequent cases have applied this criteria. For example, in *H E Dibble Ltd v. Moore* [1970] 2 Q.B. 181 (C.A.), the court decided that moveable greenhouses (standing on their own weight on dollies which were not fixed to the ground) did not pass to the new owners of the property under section 62 of the *Law of Property Act 1925; in Elwes v. Maw* (1802) 3 East. 38, a dutch barn which rested on its own sockets let into the ground was held not to be a fixture.

KEY PRINCIPLE: *The two tests set out in* Holland v. Hodgson, *are still relevant in deciding whether an item is a fixture or a fitting.*

TSB Bank plc v. Botham 1996

The court had to decide whether items such as fitted carpets, light fittings, gas fires, curtains and blinds, towel rails, soap dishes, a Victorian bath, tap fittings and shower head, mirrors attached to the walls, kitchen units, sink and electrical items such as the oven, dishwasher, integrated washing machine, extractor fan, gas hob, refrigerator and freezer were fixtures or chattels.

HELD: (C.A.) Applying the two tests set out in *Holland v. Hodgson*, the gas hob, the extractor fan, freezer, oven, dishwasher, an integrated washing machine, refrigerator, fitted carpets and curtains, gas fires and a Victorian bath standing on its four short legs were not fixtures. The other items referred to above were, however, regarded as fixtures. Lawtel. L.T.L. *August 3, 1996* (Unreported).

COMMENTARY

At first instance, the court decided that all the items were to be regarded as fixtures. This appeared to demonstrate the courts' preference for the purpose of annexation test rather than the degree of annexation test. This preference has been seen in earlier cases, as dicta from Lord Scarman in *Berkley v. Poulett* (1976) 241 E.G. 911 has suggested. In *Leigh v. Taylor* [1902] A.C. 157 (H.L.), tapestries which were affixed to the walls of a house were held to be chattels and not fixtures as the purpose of annexing them to the wall was for the better enjoyment of the chattel. In contrast, in *D'eyncourt v. Gregory* (1866) L.R. 3 E.Q. 382, it was held that marble statues of lions were held to be fixtures as their presence on the land was for the better enjoyment of the land. The first instance decision in *Botham* surprised many as it was assumed that electrical items such as freezers, and dishwashers would be chattels, which could be removed by the vendor on a conveyance of the land, in the absence of any agreement. The practical effect is that it would have increased the value of the property which the mortgagee could have obtained from the sale. The Court of Appeal has now overturned this decision and reverted back to the original tests for whether an item is a chattel or a fixture.

The two tests set out in *Holland v. Hodgson* were recently applied by the House of Lords in *Elitestone Ltd v. Morris* [1997] 1 W.L.R. 687 where their Lordships decided that a bungalow erected on pillars was a fixture!

Airspace

KEY PRINCIPLE: *The owner of land has rights over his air space. Invasion of the airspace at the lower stratum (the portion of airspace extending to about 200 metres above roof level), prima facie, amounts to a trespass.*

Kelsen v. Imperial Tobacco Co. Ltd 1957

An advertising sign erected by the defendants encroached into the airspace above the plaintiff's property. The plaintiff applied for a mandatory injunction for the removal of the sign.

HELD: (Q.B.D.) The invasion of the plaintiff's airspace amounted to a trespass and therefore a mandatory injunction would be granted.[1957] Q.B. 334.

COMMENTARY
It is clear that where there is an invasion of the lower stratum of the airspace, this amounts to trespass. It would have caused economic interference and loss of enjoyment to the owner of the land. McNair J. suggested that where there is an invasion of at a height which might interfere with the owner's use of the land, this would amount to a trespass rather than a nuisance.

KEY PRINCIPLE: *Where an injunction is granted to restrain the invasion of air space, it is generally inappropriate to suspend the injunction.*

Jaggard v. Sawyer 1995

The plaintiff brought proceedings for an injunction to restrain the defendants' breach of covenant and trespass over her part of a road. The plaintiff had earlier threatened to bring proceedings but had taken no action until some time later.

HELD: (C.A.) That since the use of the road would cause minimal damage to the plaintiff and having regard to the defendants' conduct and the plaintiff's delay in applying for an injunction, the grant of an injunction would be oppressive. In the circumstances of the case, it was appropriate to award damages in lieu of granting an injunction.

COMMENTARY

In *Anchor Brewhouse Developments Ltd v. Berkley House (Docklands Developments) Ltd* [1987] 2 E.G.L.R. 173, Scott J. granted an injunction to prevent the invasion of the land-owner's airspace by the booms of tower cranes belonging to the defendants, but suspended it for 21 days. Further, in *Woollerton and Wilson Ltd v. Richard Costain Ltd* [1970] 1 W.L.R. 411, an injunction granted on similar facts was suspended for 12 months to allow the building work to be completed. These two decisions were disapproved of in *Jaggard v. Sawyer*, which suggested that it was inappropriate to suspend the injunction in this type of case.

KEY PRINCIPLE: *Invasion of airspace in the higher stratum does not amount to an actionable trespass.*

Berstein of Leigh (Baron) v. Skyviews & General Ltd 1978

The defendants took an aerial photograph of the country house belonging to the plaintiff. They offered to sell the picture to him. The plaintiff alleged, *inter alia*, that the defendants were liable for trespass.

HELD: (Q.B.D.) That the defendants did not infringe the plaintiff's rights and therefore no trespass was committed. [1978] Q.B. 479.

COMMENTARY
Griffiths J. stated that a landowner did not have unlimited rights over his airspace. His rights over the airspace were limited to such height as was necessary for the ordinary use and enjoyment of the land. Above that height, the landowner had no better rights than any other individual.

Objects Found On or In Land

KEY PRINCIPLE: *An object or item found buried in the ground belongs to the owner of the land.*

Elwes v. Briggs Gas Co. 1886
The question arose as to whether a prehistoric boat which was buried in the soil, six feet below the surface, belonged to the owner of the land.

HELD: (Ch.D.) That the prehistoric boat which was buried in the ground belonged to the owner of the land, irregardless of the fact that the owner of the land was unaware of the existence of the boat. (1886) 33 Ch. D. 562.

Waverley Borough Council v. Fletcher 1995
The defendant, who was lawfully present in a park owned by the plaintiff, used a metal detector and found a medieval gold brooch which was buried in the ground. The plaintiff had a policy of prohibiting the use of metal detectors in the park which the defendant was unaware of. The brooch was held by a coroner's court not to be treasure trove and returned to the defendant. The plaintiff commenced an action against the defendant to claim the brooch.

HELD: (C.A.) That where an object was found in or attached to the land, the owner of the land had a better title to the object that the finder. In the circumstances, the plaintiff's appeal against the first instance decision would be allowed.[1995] 3 W.L.R. 772.

COMMENTARY
Both these cases make it clear that where an item or object is found buried or attached to the ground, the owner of the land has a better claim to it as against the finder. In such a situation, there is no need for the owner of the land to have manifested any intention to retain control over such items or objects. It was also irrelevant whether the finder was a trespasser or a lawful invitee onto the land.

KEY PRINCIPLE: *Where the object or item found buried in the ground amounts to treasure trove, the rightful owner is the Crown. This principle is now subject to the Treasure Act 1996.*

Attorney General of the Duchy of Lancaster v. G.E. Overton (Farms) Ltd 1982

A hoard of about 7,811 Roman coins were discovered buried in a field in Lincolnshire. A coroner's court found that they were treasure trove and therefore belonged to the crown. The defendants claimed that the hoard was not treasure trove as it did not consist of silver coins.

HELD: (Ch.D.) That the Crown's right to claim treasure trove did not extend to items not made of gold or silver. It was a question of fact for the court to decide whether a coin was a silver coin and in reaching that decision, the court was not compelled to apply any rigid rule as to the required silver content. On the facts of the case, the coins were not treasure trove. [1981] 1 Ch. 333.

COMMENTARY

The importance of this case is that it clarifies the position as to what amounts to treasure trove. Dillon J. suggested that treasure trove is when the object contain a substantial amount of gold or silver, is concealed in the land, and the owner is unknown. However, this rule is now subject to the *Treasure Act 1996*.

The *Treasure Act 1996* received royal assent on 4th July 1996 but at the time of writing, no date had been fixed for its implementation. The Act abolishes treasure trove and replaces it with the term treasure and new rules relating to it. section 1 of the Act defines treasure as any object which is at least 300 years old, which if not a coin has a metal content of at 10 per cent silver or gold. Where the find concerns a coin, it will be regarded as treasure if it is one of at least two coins having a metal content of least 10 per cent silver or gold or where it is one of at least ten coins, both of which must be at least 300 years old. Section 4 of the *Treasure Act 1996* provides that when treasure is found, subject to prior interests and rights, it would vest in the franchisee (as defined in section 5 of the Act), if there is one, otherwise it vests in the Crown. The Act also makes provision for the holding of inquests in the coroners court (section 7) and makes it a summary offence of failing to report the find to the coroner (section 8). The other important part of the Act relates to the payment of a reward, where the Secretary of State determines that a reward is payable. Section 10 expressly provides that the reward may be paid to the finder or the occupier of the land on which the item is found or any other person having an interest in the land. The Secretary of State is directed by section 11 of the Act to prepare a code of practice relating to treasure.

KEY PRINCIPLE: *An object or item found on the ground belongs to the finder unless the owner of the land manifested his intention to retain control over such items or the finder is a trespasser.*

Parker v. British Airways Board 1982

The plaintiff was in the international executive lounge at terminal one of Heathrow Airport when he found a gold bracelet lying on the floor. He gave it to the defendant's employee with his name and address and made it clear that if the owner of the bracelet did not claim it, it should be returned to him. As there was no claimant for the bracelet, the defendant sold it and retained the proceeds. The plaintiff claimed the proceeds of sale from the defendant.

HELD: (C.A.) The plaintiff acquired rights of possession of the bracelet by having taken it into his care and control. The defendant could have better rights to the bracelet if they manifested an intention to exercise control over the airport lounge and things in it. As the defendant failed to manifest such an intention, it had no rights over the bracelet, as such, the proceeds of sale had to be given to the plaintiff. [1982] 1 Q.B. 1004.

COMMENTARY

It is clear that where a person is an invitee onto the land, any objects found on the property by that person will belong to him, unless the owner of the land has made it clear that any such objects found on the land belongs to him. This intention must be manifested prior to the objects being found, for example, by a notice stating clearly that items found on the premises would not be returned. The court also suggested that where the finder is a trespasser, his or her rights are frail.

In such a case the owner of the land has a better claim to the objects found on the land.

Ownership of Wild Animals and Fish Found on the Property

KEY PRINCIPLE: *The owner of the land has a qualified property in wild animals and fish which are found within the boundaries of his land.*

Blade v. Higgs 1865

The plaintiff chased and killed rabbits on land belonging to the Marquis of Exeter without permission. He sold these rabbits to a third party.

HELD: (H.L.) That the servants of the Marquis were entitled to take possession of the dead rabbits as they belonged to the Marquis.(1865) 11 H.L. Cas. 621.

COMMENTARY

This means that the owner of the land has the right to hunt and catch the wild animals or fish (unless they are protected species) and once they are caught and killed, he acquires ownership of them. See also *Nicholls v. Ely Beet Sugar Factory Ltd* [1933] 1 Ch. 343.

---

2. PROTECTION OF INTERESTS IN LAND

Introduction

The estates and interests capable of existing at law are set out in section 1 of the *Law of Property Act 1925*. Whether the estate or interest in fact takes effect in law depends on its required mode of creation and registration. See Chap. 3 on the Formal and Informal Methods of Acquisition of Interests in Land.

Upon the sale of land it is necessary to have a system for protecting third party interests in that land. Historically, there have been three stages of development in protecting third party interests.

Prior to any system of registration, legal rights bound the world whilst equitable rights bound all except a bona fide purchaser for value of a legal estate without notice.

In the unregistered land system, the above prevailed except that certain interests were registrable as Land Charges. Protection of such interests depended on their registration.

In the registered land system, estates are substantively registrable, mortgages need to be protected as registered charges, certain interests are specified as being overriding without needing registration, the remainder of interests should be entered on the register as minor interests in order to be protected.

Unregistered Title

KEY PRINCIPLE: *Historically, protection of equitable interests has depended on the doctrine of notice.*

Jones v. Smith 1841

The mortgagee enquired of the mortgagor as to interests affecting the security offered. The mortgagee was informed that the marriage settlement included only the wife's property and not the husband's estate being offered as security. The mortgagee advanced money without seeing the settlement which in fact did include the husband's estate.

HELD: (Ch.D.) The mortgagee was not affected with constructive notice of the settlement's true contents. Constructive notice applies in two cases: first, where the party has notice that the property is encumbered or in some way affected, then he is deemed to have knowledge of facts to which he would have been led by due enquiry from the knowledge he actually had: secondly, where the party had a suspicion that the land was charged and wilfully or fraudulently determined to avoid receiving actual notice thereof. (1841) 1 Hare 43.

COMMENTARY
A purchaser is caught by notice of prior interests. Sufficient knowledge can be actual knowledge, constructive knowledge as described in this case or imputed knowledge i.e. knowledge attributed to the purchaser by the actual or constructive knowledge of one's legal representative. Compare *Hunt v. Luck* [1901] 1 Ch. 45 where it was held that knowledge

that rents were paid to an estate agent did not constitute notice of an intermediate interest adverse to the vendor.

KEY PRINCIPLE: *A transferee takes free of a prior interest of which he has no knowledge.*

Pilcher v. Rawlins 1872

The mortgagor conveyed land to trustees of a settlement in return for trust money. The surviving trustee later conveyed part of the land back in return for part-payment of the loan which he then misappropriated. The mortgagor then conveyed that part of the land to new mortgagees concealing, with the trustee's connivance, the prior mortgage and re-conveyance. The beneficiaries of the trust sought to recover the unpaid debt by asserting that the new mortgagees took subject to the original mortgage.

HELD: (C.A.) The new mortgagees took the estate free of the prior interests. (1872) 7 Ch. App. 259.

COMMENTARY
The original conveyance recorded the terms of the trust. The subsequent conveyance did not, so it appeared to the new mortgagees that the land was unencumbered.

KEY PRINCIPLE: *An interest which fails to bind a purchaser is also destroyed for the purposes of subsequent owners of the land.*

Wilkes v. Spooner 1911

The lessee of 137 High Street, East Ham, carried on the business of pork butcher and covenanted not to carry on any other business there other than a pork butcher. He was also lessee of 170 High Street, East Ham, under a different landlord where he carried on the business of general butcher. He assigned No. 170 covenanting with the plaintiff that in effect he and his successors would not use No. 137 to compete as general butchers. He surrendered the lease of No. 137 to the landlord who then leased it to the now former lessee's son. The lease contained a covenant not to carry on any business other than a butcher (not specifying pork butcher as before). At the time of the surrender the landlord was not aware of the covenant made with the plaintiff, though the son was.

HELD: (C.A.) The landlord was not affected with constructive notice when he acquired back the lease. The grant to the son of a new lease was thus free of any such restriction and the son could carry on business as a general butcher.[1911] 2 K.B. 473.

COMMENTARY

Whilst apparently unfair on the facts, this case makes clear the destructive effect of a conveyance (in this case a surrender) upon unprotected interests. This serves the interests of certainty of dealings in that subsequent owners of the land will not get caught up in old and undiscoverable interests which could effect the use and value of the land.

KEY PRINCIPLE: *To be registrable, an interest in land must be proprietary and not just personal.*

Pritchard v. Briggs 1980

In 1944 L. and his wife sold a hotel and surrounding land to R retaining a house, lake and petrol pumps. The sale contained a covenant to the purchaser and successors that so long as the vendors and purchaser were alive, the vendors and successors would not sell the retained land without giving the purchaser an option to buy the retained land. The covenant was registered under the *Land Charges Act 1925*. In 1947 R sold the hotel with the benefit of the covenant to M, who similarly sold on the land to the first and second defendants in 1954. In 1953 L and his wife had granted a weekly lease of the retained land other than the house to the plaintiff. In 1959 a five-year lease was granted to the plaintiff with a covenant that the plaintiff would have the option to buy all the retained lands upon giving notice within three months after the death of the survivor of L and his wife. In 1964 a further lease of 25 years was granted also containing the option. The option was registered under the *Land Charges Act 1925*.

The wife died, L's health deteriorated, and funds were urgently needed for looking after him. His nephew, the third defendant, was appointed receiver and with the authority of the Court of Protection agreed to sell the retained lands to the first and second defendants in pursuance of the 1944 pre-emption, conditional upon them indemnifying L and his nephew against any claim by the plaintiff. L died and the land was conveyed to the first and second defendants. The plaintiff served notice purporting to exercise his option.

HELD: (C.A.) A right of pre-emption grants no proprietary right in land. There was no right to call for a sale until the grantor satisfied the conditions of the grant. The pre-emption could only bind once the conditions were satisfied. The registration of the option which was proprietary right took priority over the pre-emption. [1980] Ch. 338.

COMMENTARY
The registration of the pre-emption was therefore ineffective. A pre-emption could only be effectively registered once the conditions of the pre-emption were met. This will be impractical if other rights have been granted and registered in the meantime.

KEY PRINCIPLE: *An option is a registrable interest at the time of its grant and binds subsequent purchasers when registered.*

Armstrong & Holmes v. Holmes 1993
In 1986 the first defendant granted the plaintiff an option to buy land. This was subsequently registered under the *Land Charges Act 1972*. The plaintiff sought to exercise the option but the first defendant would not co-operate in setting a price. The first defendant sold part of the land to a third-party subject to the option insofar as it subsisted. The third party then sold that part of the land to the second defendant subject to the option.

HELD: (Ch.D.) The second defendant took subject to the option. The option was a registrable interest and had been protected by registration. The exercise of the option was not a separately registrable interest. [1993] 1W.L.R. 1482.

COMMENTARY
The case represents the converse of *Pritchard v. Briggs* [1980] Ch. 338 (see above) in two senses. Firstly, an option is registrable upon grant but a pre-emption is registrable only when it becomes exercisable. Secondly, an unprotected inter-

est is extinguished in respect of subsequent owners of land whereas a protected interest binds such owners. In *Phillips v. Mobil Oil Co. Ltd.* [1989] 1 W.L.R. 888 it was held that an option to re-new a lease was a registrable estate contract and failure to protect it by registration made it void as against a purchaser of the land.

KEY PRINCIPLE: *A right of re-entry is an independent proprietary right but was not required to be registered as a land charge.*

Shiloh Spinners v. Harding 1973

The plaintiffs assigned their lease in a mill to T Ltd, who made covenants as to fencing and support. The plaintiffs had a right of re-entry in respect of breaches of covenants. This right of re-entry was not registered as a land charge. T Ltd assigned the lease to the defendant. By the terms of the lease to T Ltd, they would not be liable for breaches made by their successors. The defendant was in breach and the plaintiff sought to exercise the right of re-entry.

HELD: (H.L.) A right of re-entry can subsist as an independent proprietary right unconnected to an interest in a reversion. Such a right did not fall under those required to be registered under the *Land Charges Act 1925.* [1973] A.C. 691.

COMMENTARY
The right of re-entry thus bound the defendant without the need for registration. The court could have exercised equitable jurisdiction to grant relief against forfeiture but did not because the breaches were wilful and continuous.

KEY PRINCIPLE: *An easement arising by estoppel on the grounds of mutual benefit and burden and acquiescence is not required to be registered and binds successors to the land.*

E R Ives Investment v. High 1967

The defendant's neighbour, W, built foundations which encroached into the substratum of the defendant's land. It was orally agreed that the defendant would allow this trespass to continue and that W would allow the defendant to have a right of way across W's backyard to get access to a side road. W sold his property to purchasers who knew of the agreement.

The defendant built a garage which could only be used in conjunction with the right of way. The purchasers made no objection to the garage or use of the right of way. They got the defendant to resurface the yard for which he paid one fifth of the cost. The property was sold to the plaintiffs. Both the auction notice and the conveyance said that the sale was subject to the right of way. The right of way was never registered as a land charge. The plaintiffs sought a declaration that the right of way was void against them for want of registration and asked for damages and injunction for the alleged trespass.

HELD: (C.A.) By the mutual benefit and burden and acquiescence there was an estoppel based easement which was not required to be registered as a land charge. [1967] 2 Q.B. 379.

COMMENTARY
On the evidence there would clearly have been unjust to deny the defendants' right of way. It would not be logical to demand a right be registered where its existence comes about by estoppel.

KEY PRINCIPLE: *A spouse's right of occupation under the* Matrimonial Homes Act 1983 *is strictly not a proprietary right but can be registered as a land charge. Its registration stalls dealings in the land until family law issues are resolved.*

Wroth v. Tyler 1974

The defendant agreed to sell his bungalow with vacant possession to the plaintiff. Before completion his wife entered a notice on the Register of her right of occupation under the *Matrimonial Homes Act 1967*. The plaintiff sought specific performance and/or damages.

HELD: (Ch.D.) To grant specific performance with vacant possession would require the husband to litigate against his wife. To grant specific performance with the wife in occupation would split the family, not protect the defendant or daughter and would leave the wife open to eviction once the purchase was complete. The court granted damages in lieu of specific performance to the value of the difference between the offer price and current value. [1974] 1 Ch. 30.

COMMENTARY
Whilst strictly not a property right but a personal one, a spouse's right of occupation has the characteristic of a charge on the property when registered. This then binds future purchasers of the property.

KEY PRINCIPLE: *Failure to register an estate contract does not matter as between the parties but leaves the agreement void as against purchasers.*

Hollington Bros v. Rhodes 1951

Seven-year underleases were agreed between the defendant landlord and the plaintiffs. Documents were signed but not formally completed. The agreements were not registered as land charges. The defendant assigned the head lease to D subject to tenancies which may affect the property. D served notice arguing that the plaintiffs only enjoyed periodic annual tenancies. The plaintiffs had to renegotiate new leases of the full term at a higher rent and with a premium payable. The plaintiffs sought a declaration that they were entitled to the original lease agreed and damages for failure to complete that agreement.

HELD: (Ch.D.) The contract had never been completed. Had there been a contract they would have been entitled to their claim to damages against the defendant. [1951] 2 T.L.R. 691.

COMMENTARY
There is no obligation to register an interest. As between grantor and grantee it is binding in contract law without the need for registration. However, failure to register makes the agreement void as to successors to the property.

Key Principle: *An unprotected interest falling under class C(iv) or D of the* Land Charges Act 1972 *will not survive a sale to a purchaser for money or money's worth. Such a purchaser need not act in good faith nor have to provide a commercial price as long as there is valuable consideration.*

Midland Bank Trust Co. Ltd v. Green 1981

A father granted his son an option to buy a property. The son
did not register his estate contract. The father conveyed the
land to his wife for £500 when the property was worth
£40,000, almost twice the fixed sum which the option was
set at. The conveyance was done with some haste and secrecy.
On the evidence the sale was made in order to defeat to the
unprotected option. The son purported to exercise the option
but the mother refused to sell. The son sought a declaration
that the option was binding. By the time the case reached the
House of Lords the property was worth £400,000. The dispute
became one between the son's widow and children against his
parents estate. The difference in the widow and childrens'
inheritance would be huge depending on the outcome of the
case.

HELD: (H.L.) The House of Lords overruled the Court of
Appeal and found that the mother had taken free of the son's
unprotected interest. To take free of an unprotected interest
such as this, section 13(2) of the *Land Charges Act 1925*, now
section 4(6) of the 1972 Act, requires that there be a purchaser
for money or money's worth. Money or money's worth did not
have to be a fair commercial price but merely valuable consideration. This could even be nominal consideration. The
meaning of purchaser did not, according to the statute, require
that the purchase be in good faith. This requirement was one of
the problems in the old system of discerning motive and intention which the Act sought to remove. [1981] A.C. 513.

COMMENTARY

The decision may look unfair given the apparent intention to
take advantage of the son. However, in the long run justice is
served better by a system which provides for certainty of
dealings. The answer to plaintiffs in such a position of the
son is to register your interest. Failure to do so will otherwise
lead to people taking a legal advantage of one's careless-
ness. It is not a fraud to take legal advantage of another's
failings. A similar conclusion was reached in *Lloyds Bank v.
Carrick* [1996] 4 All E.R. 630.

KEY PRINCIPLE: *In unregistered land a purchaser takes free
of beneficial interests of which he has no notice, actual, constructive or imputed.*

Caunce v. Caunce 1969

A husband and wife agreed to buy a house in their joint names with the help of a loan. Without the wife's knowledge the husband had the house put in his sole name and obtained three different bank loans using the house as security. The husband was declared bankrupt and he left the matrimonial home. The wife who stayed in the home sought declarations that:

[i] the husband held the home on trust for herself and the banks;

[ii] the banks' mortgages were charged only against the husband's beneficial interest;

[iii] her interest had priority over that of the banks;

[iv] the bank who were also her bankers had constructive notice of her equitable interest.

HELD: (Ch.D.) The bank took free of her interest unless they had constructive notice of it. An enquiry into the wife's account was not an enquiry that the bank ought reasonably have made and there were no special facts which should have brought to their notice her interest. Mortgagees were not affected with notice of equitable interests of people residing in the property where that residence was not inconsistent with the title offered as security. They were not fixed with constructive knowledge by failure to enquire. The mere fact of it being a matrimonial home did not raise a need to enquire. [1969] 1 W.L.R. 286.

COMMENTARY

Section 199 of the Law of Property Act 1925 provides in effect that a purchaser (section 87 puts a mortgagee in the same position) takes free of interests of which he has no actual or constructive notice. The case implies that a bank need not go behind the circumstances of a matrimonial home held in the name of one spouse. As the land was unregistered title no claim could be made to an overriding interest. Compare this with the recent shift in the courts' attitude towards the degree to which a bank should enquire as to beneficial interests in property. (See Chap. 8 on Mortgages).

Registered Title

In the Registered Title system the estate is substantively registered. Third-party interests are either entered on the register against the substantive registration or are overriding i.e. interests defined in section 70 of the *Land Registration Act 1925* as binding without the need for any registration. Legal mortgages are entered as Registered Charges. All other interests not being substantively registrable estates, Registered Charges or overriding interests should be entered on the register as minor interests in the form of a notice, inhibition, restriction or caution.

[a] Registered charges

KEY PRINCIPLE: *Registration normally determines the survival of an interest but the general rule that where equities are equal the first in time prevails can still apply.*

Mortgage Corporation Ltd v. Nationwide Credit Corporation Ltd 1994

The registered owners executed a legal charge in favour of the plaintiffs in return for a loan of £367,500. The plaintiffs did not enter this as a registered charge or protect it as a minor interest. The proprietors executed a second mortgage in return for a loan of £60,000 from the defendants. This was entered as a notice under section 49 of the *Land Registration Act 1925*. As the proceeds of sale were insufficient to meet both loans the issue arose as to which mortgage had priority.

HELD: (C.A.) A charge protected by notice only takes effect in equity until entered as a registered charge. Section 52 of the *Land Registration Act 1925* provides that a disposition takes effect subject to interests protected by notice except where they are defeated independently of the Act by another disposition. The first mortgage, also unregistered, takes effect in equity. The second mortgage taking effect in equity (albeit entered as a notice) lost priority to the earlier mortgage. [1994] Ch. 49.

COMMENTARY

The decision reflects the general principle that where equities are equal, the first in time prevails. It is anomalous, however, that the second mortgagee suffered having done all he could do whereas the first had not protected his interest by registration. This is one example of the incompleteness of the registration system. In *Barclays Bank v. Taylor* [1974] Ch. 137, the plaintiff had a mortgage in the land protected by caution but not entered as a registered charge. The plaintiff later contracted to buy the land and entered a caution. The Court of Appeal held that the mortgage and estate contract both took effect in equity and the *Land Registration Act 1925* did not effect priority, so the earlier in time took priority.

[b] Minor interests

KEY PRINCIPLE: *A contractual interest relating to property cannot be protected by registration.*

Lynton International Ltd. v. Noble 1991

The plaintiff purchaser of a property agreed with the defendant vendor to pay a certain proportion of the resale price to the defendant. The defendant entered a caution hoping to protect his interest in the proceeds of the resale.

HELD: (Ch.D.) The caution would be vacated. This was a purely contractual matter. An interest under a trust for sale is protectable. There was, however, no disposition or settlement creating a trust but an agreement as to what would happen when or if the property was sold. [1991] 63 P.&C.R. 452.

COMMENTARY
A caution puts a hold on dealings in land but should be used to protect interests in land not claims against owners of land. See also *Pritchard v. Briggs*, above and *National Provincial Bank Ltd. v. Hastings Car Mart Ltd.*, below. Note also the effect of the *Trusts of Land and Appointment of Trustees Act 1996* which replaces the "trust for sale" with the "trust of land" (see Chap. 5).

KEY PRINCIPLE: *A cautioner who consents to a grant of a legal charge cannot later prevent dealings in the land by the chargee.*

Chancery plc v. Ketteringham 1993

Property developers agreed to grant a lease to the defendant in consideration of £95,000. A caution was entered in the defendant's name. The developers negotiated a loan from the plaintiff for £570,000. The plaintiff asked for and received from the defendant consent for a mortgage of the freehold to be granted. The mortgage was duly entered as a Registered Charge. The defendant went into occupation though a lease had not formally been granted. The plaintiff now sought to enforce its charge free of the defendant's lease agreement.

HELD: (Ch.D.) The proprietor of a legal charge entered on the register with the consent of a cautioner could deal with the land free of the rights of that cautioner. [1993] T.L.R. 954.

COMMENTARY
Whilst apparently harsh, it is almost certainly true that the plaintiff would not have exposed himself to risk without obtaining the defendant's consent.

KEY PRINCIPLE: *A notice of deposit of a land certificate can be construed as a caution taking priority over later cautions even when the notice of execution of equitable mortgage based on the deposit is not yet made.*

In re White Rose Cottage 1965

The proprietors of land deposited the land certificate and executed a memorandum of deposit with a bank as security for a loan. In May 1962 a notice of deposit was entered on the register. Creditors of the proprietors obtained charging orders and lodged cautions on the Register in June and August 1962. In August 1962 the bank applied to enter a notice on the register of the equitable charge created by the memorandum. The creditors objected, claiming that their notices should have priority. In October 1962 the bank sold the land to a purchaser who on the same day executed a mortgage in favour of a building society. The creditors again claimed the sale and mortgage should be subject to their notices' priority.

HELD: (C.A.) The bank's notice of deposit took effect as a caution and had priority over the creditors' charges. The creditors could not object to the registration by the bank of their charge. The sale was construed as being by the proprietor with the consent of the bank so that the purchaser got the same title as the former proprietor free of the bank's mortgage but subject to the creditors' charges. [1965] 2 W.L.R. 337.

COMMENTARY
The case is an example of the problems of multiple modes of protection of minor interests. To say that notice of deposit acts as a caution seems to prejudice a subsequent cautioner who

suffers by a subsequent registration of a notice of an equitable charge. The effect is that the mortgage loan is recovered from the proceeds but the creditors charges are not so repaid although they do bind the purchaser. The construction of the sale is also arguable because a sale by an equitable mortgagee acting under his power of sale could not have conveyed the full legal estate.

KEY PRINCIPLE: *An unregistered minor interest may bind a fraudulent transferee. Mere knowledge of the fact of non-registration does not amount to fraud.*

Peffer v. Rigg 1977

In 1962 the plaintiff and first defendant bought a house as an investment and home for the first defendant's mother-in law. The house was put into the first defendant's name to be held on trust for the plaintiff and first defendant. The house was divided into two flats. The lower one was occupied by their mother-in-law and the upper one was rented out. The rental income covered the loan repayments on the house. The first defendant's wife moved into the lower flat. The plaintiff was concerned at this. An express trust was drawn up to reflect the original agreement. Further lettings of the upper flat became problematic as it would involve granting a protected tenancy. The first defendant, however, re–let the upper flat without the plaintiff's knowledge. The first defendant and his wife divorced. As part of the settlement he transferred the freehold of the house to her purporting to do so as beneficial owner and for consideration of £1. It was intended that she took over the mortgage repayments from the letting income from the upper flat. The plaintiff claimed that the re–letting of the upper flat and selling of the freehold were in breach of trust. He also contended that the second defendant, the first defendant's ex-wife, held the house on trust 50 per cent for the plaintiff. She denied knowledge of any interest of the plaintiff and claimed that no trust was registered and that she paid valuable consideration. The first defendant denied breach of trust in the re–letting and claimed that he had only sold his interest in the house.

HELD: (Ch.D.) The re–letting was not in breach of trust. The first defendant acted reasonably as rental income was needed to cover the shortfall caused by the plaintiff's refusal to contribute maintenance of the house. The second defendant knew that the property had been held on trust. If the consideration was regarded as nominal then under section 20(4) she took the house subject to the plaintiff's unregistered interest. If there was valuable consideration in the context of the overall divorce settlement, it was still a requirement under sections 20 and 59 for the second defendant to be a purchaser in good faith. Even then, as she knew the property was held on trust she took it on general equitable grounds under a constructive trust for herself and the plaintiff. [1977] 1 W.L.R. 285.

COMMENTARY

The express trust which bound the first defendant may have needed registration to bind purchasers generally. The constructive trust affecting the conscience of the purchaser in this case could not be registered in advance and could not be required to be registered. Cases like this illustrate the vital need to formalise arrangements at the start especially in family dealings. It also illustrates the need in extreme cases for courts to find exceptions to the general requirement to register to protect beneficial interests by entry as minor interests. However, the implication that more than nominal consideration is required is dubious, because what is valuable consideration is in the eye of the beholder not the eye of the judge. The requirement of good faith alluded to in this case is also doubtful. Fraud is a clear defence against failure to register. However, knowledge or even taking advantage of another's lack of care is not equal to fraud.

Beneficial Interests

Beneficial interests can be registered as minor interests and will bind a transferee if registered unless removed. A beneficial interest in land is overreached by payment to two trustees thus converting the interest into one in the proceeds rather than the land. A beneficial interest if not overreached can be the foundation for an overriding interest if there is also actual occupation.

KEY PRINCIPLE: *Where a beneficial interest is overreached an interest in the property is converted into an interest in the* *proceeds and can thereafter not be used as the basis of an overriding interest of actual occupation.*

City of London Building Society v. Flegg 1987

A couple bought a house for £34,000 for themselves and the wife's parents to reside in. The parents contributed £18,000. The remainder was to be raised by the couple from a loan. The couple were registered as proprietors and as joint beneficial tenants under a trust for sale. The parents lived in the house. The couple executed two further mortgages without the knowledge of the wife's parents. Then all three charges were discharged by an advance by the plaintiffs of £37,500 in return for another mortgage. No enquiries were made of the wife's parents. The couple defaulted and the plaintiff took repossession proceedings. The parents claimed a prior beneficial interest by virtue of their contribution to the purchase price. They also claimed that their interests plus occupation at the time of execution of the plaintiff's mortgage gave them an overriding interest.

HELD: (H.L.) The parents' interest were overreached by the payment which was properly made to two trustees. Given that their beneficial interest in the house was overreached, they no longer had a property interest upon which an overriding interest of actual occupation could be based. [1987] 2 W.L.R. 1266.

COMMENTARY

The 1925 legislation sought to balance the need to protect beneficiaries with the need to make land alienable when held under a trust. Once the wife's parents' interests had been overreached they had no separate interest in the house which could effect the mortgagees. Their claim should lie against the trustees. They should not be in a better situation than a beneficiary who happens not to be in residence. Whilst the principle confirmed by the House of Lords in this case seems to be a clear and sensible application of section 2(1)(ii), it was not always the way courts went previously.

[c] Overriding Interests

KEY PRINCIPLE: *A beneficial interest, albeit unregistered, can form the basis for an overriding interest of actual occupation where the transferee fails to make enquiries.*

Williams & Glyns Bank Ltd v. Boland 1980

The case merges two actions on materially the same facts. A husband was a registered proprietor of a house. The wife had contributed a large part of the purchase price and the mortgage loan repayments. She therefore had a beneficial interest in the house. He mortgaged the house to the bank, who made no enquiries of the wife. The house was the matrimonial home in which husband and wife resided. The loan was defaulted upon and a possession order was granted.

HELD: (H.L.) The wife had an overriding interest of actual occupation under s.70(1)(g) of the *Land Registration Act 1925*, to which the bank's interest was subject. Her actual occupation based upon her beneficial interest was more than just a minor interest. Of itself a beneficial interest is registrable as a minor interest. If not registered, a minor interest does not by section 3 (xv) affect a purchaser. [1980] A.C. 487.

COMMENTARY

In *City of London v. Flegg* [1987] 2 W.L.R. 1266 (see above) the wife's parents beneficial interest was overreached thus leaving them nothing upon which to base actual occupation. In the present case the beneficial interest was not over-reached by payment to two trustees so it made a foundation for occupation. The actual occupation then became overriding because the mortgage was executed without the bank making enquiries, resulting in them losing priority to the wife. This case made it clear to lenders that they must check for possible overriding interests and cannot rely on no beneficial interest being registered. *Flegg* makes it clear that lenders are safest by advancing monies to two trustees.

KEY PRINCIPLE: *An overriding interest of actual occupation must be founded on a proprietary right of some kind. The rights of a deserted wife are personal.*

Lloyds Bank v. Rosset 1991

A couple wished to purchase a semi-derelict house as their home. As the purchase price was to be paid out of the husband's trust fund, its trustees insisted that the legal title be in the husband's sole name. The vendors allowed the purchasers access to the property before the exchange of contracts. Renovation work was commenced with the wife carrying out some-

decorating work as well as undertaking the supervision of the builders. The husband took out an overdraft with the plaintiffs to cover the renovation costs.Upon the husband's default of the loan, the plaintiffs sought possession of the property.

HELD: (H.L.) The wife's activities in respect of the renovation work prior to completion did not provide sufficient evidence on which the court could infer a common intention that she should have a beneficial interest in the property. In the absence of any express common intention, the finding that the husband held the property as constructive trustee for himself and his wife could not be supported. [1991] 1 A.C. 107.

National Provincial Bank Ltd v. Hastings Car Mart Ltd 1965
See Chap. 7 on Licences.

COMMENTARY
Contractual licences and equities should not be regarded as proprietary rights which form the basis of an overriding interest. The reasoning is that these are rights enforceable against the person, which should not bind the land. However, the extension of ways in which rights in land can be acquired does make the possibility of unforseen overriding interests arising greater. This may particularly be the case where the origin of the interests lies in the acts of parties which may not be apparent to a purchaser, but, who may be bound by an overriding interest on which there was no obvious cause to enquire about.

The law recognizes for example, in *Hammond v. Mitchell* [1992] 2 All E.R. 109 that beneficial interests can be impliedly acquired by cohabitees where there is an agreement or understanding that property be beneficially shared upon which the claimant has detrimentally relied giving rise to a constructive trust or proprietary estoppel.This decision followed *Lloyds Bank v. Rosset*. It should be noted that Lord Bridge stated in *Rosset*, that in the absence of any express common intention, it was doubtful if any conduct short of direct financial contribution will be sufficient to infer a common intention to share the property beneficially. The Court of Appeal in *Drake V. Whipp* [1996] 1 F.L.R. 826 recently emphasised that the latter gave rise to a resulting trust whilst the former was a constructive trust. The importance of this distinction is that in the case of a resulting trust, the cohabitee or spouse's share of the beneficial interest is in direct proportion to his or her contribution (*Midland Bank v. Cooke* [1995] 4 All E.R. 562, a case which suggests to the contrary, is to be doubted). In the case of a constructive trust, the court can adopt a "broad brush approach" in determing the cohabitee or spouse's share of the beneficial interest in the property.

In *Skipton Building Society v. Clayton* (1993) 66 P.&C.R. 223, it was held that a couple who had been promised a right to occupy rent free for the rest of their life had a tenancy rather than a licence.

KEY PRINCIPLE: *An overriding interest cannot be claimed where the interest upon which it is founded does not itself have priority over the transferee.*

Paddington Building Society v. Mendelsohn 1985

A mother and son agreed to buy a flat. The mother contributed roughly half the purchase price. The flat was put in the son's name so that he could raise a loan for the remainder of the purchase price in return for mortgaging the flat to the building society. The society had no knowledge of the mother. The son and girlfriend moved into the house in July. The mother moved into the flat in August and the mortgage was registered in October. The son defaulted and the society obtained a possession order. The mother claimed that she had an overriding interest of actual occupation.

HELD: (C.A.) Without any express trust or agreement at the time of the purchase, the intention must be imputed to the mother and son that her interest could not take priority over the first mortgagee. This is because they both knew that they could not buy the flat without the loan from the building society. The mother could not claim an overriding interest against the mortgagee because although she was in occupation at the relevant time (by the law prevailing then and since changed by *Abbey National v. Cann* below), the beneficial interest upon which she founded her occupation impliedly ceded priority to the bank. [1985] 50 P.&C.R. 244.

COMMENTARY

The fact of occupation does not improve any interest upon which it is alleged to be based. One cannot claim against the lender who enables you to acquire the property. Cases on overriding interests usually involve situations where a prior beneficial interest exists.

KEY PRINCIPLE: *An overriding interest can be acquired by section 70(1)(a) in relation to an equitable easement.*

Celsteel Ltd v. Alton House Holdings Ltd 1985

A development included flats at the basement and ground floor levels. An area was left for a petrol filling station. Leases to the plaintiffs contained vehicular rights of way from the road to the relevant garages or parking spaces. The third plaintiff had an agreement for such a lease and moved in though the lease was never executed. These leases were made with the first defendant's predecessor. Three years later the first defendant leased the ground floor to the second defendant, an oil company, for use as a petrol station with a car wash, shop and storage area. The leased area included part of the driveway over which the plaintiffs had right of way. It was proposed that the car wash be built in such away that the access was blocked. The plaintiffs were not made aware of the likely future use of the ground floor when they took up their leases of the flats. The plaintiffs objected to the proposed blockage of their right of way.

HELD: (Ch.D.) The car wash would cause an actionable interference. The third plaintiff's right of way was an equitable easement (not having been formally executed) not protected by entry on the register. It was, however, a right which was openly exercised and enjoyed. By rule 258 of the Land Registration Rules this took effect as an overriding interest not requiring entry on the register under section 70(1)(a). The second defendant was thus bound. The first defendant was also bound having taken the land subject to the rights (including the easement) of every person in actual occupation. The third defendant was in actual occupation. The proviso in section 70(1)(g) that the transferee is not bound where enquiry is made of such person and the rights are not disclosed did not help the defendants as they had failed to make such enquiry. [1985] W.L.R. 204.

COMMENTARY

Section 70(1)(a) was interpreted in such a way to infer that there are some equitable easements not required to be registered. Openly exercised and enjoyed rights of way could justly fall into this category as they would have been seen by the purchaser. This, however, goes against the ethos of a registration system and re-introduces an element of notice in dealings with land. Previously it was thought that the section referred to legal easements only. This has been followed by the Court of Appeal in *Thatcher v. Douglas* (1996) 146 N.L.J. 282.

KEY PRINCIPLE: *An overriding interest can be acquired by section 70(1)(f) in relation to rights acquired under the Limitation Acts.*

Bridges v. Mees 1957

The plaintiff and defendant were neighbours. In 1936 the plaintiff bought a plot of land at the rear of each of the party's land. The purchase was by oral agreement and no caution was entered to protect. In 1956 the defendant purchased the same land from a liquidator who warranted only to be trustee of title. The defendant sought possession and the plaintiff claimed to have an overriding interest having rights acquired under the Limitation Acts.

HELD: (Ch.D.) The defendant bought the estate in fee simple but subject to any overriding interests. The property was held on trust by the vendor for the plaintiff. No other beneficiary could or did sue for possession. The period of limitation could run in favour of the plaintiff. The plaintiff therefore did have an overriding interest of rights acquired under the Limitation Acts. [1957] Ch. 475.

COMMENTARY
See Chap. 3 on Formal and Informal Methods of Acquisition of Interests in Land with regard to Adverse Possession. This kind of overriding interest gives effect to claims of adverse possession where the limitation period has expired in that it frustrates an attempt by the title owner to deal with the land once the period is up. Once the period is up the register can be rectified to install the acquirer as title owner. Whether this process can be used to protect someone who acquires an interest by oral contract is dubious. The implication that an oral contract is overriding without need for protection by caution is unhelpful. It might be better to say that rights acquired under the Limitation Acts whether by adverse possession or oral contract can become overriding.

In *Chowood v. Lyall No.2* [1930] 2 Ch. 156 a squatter's rights which became overriding by effect of the Limitation Acts were recognized by rectification of the Register. See *Epps v. Esso Petroleum Co. Ltd.* [1973] W.L.R. 1071 (below).

KEY PRINCIPLE: *An overriding interest of actual occupation or receipt of rents can be acquired under section 70(1)(g).*

Strand Securities Ltd v. Caswell 1965

In 1949 the freeholders granted the first defendant's wife a lease of 42 years. In 1952 she granted a sublease of just over 39 years to the first defendant. This was not registered nor was a notice entered against the head lease. Later in 1952 the wife transferred her lease to Critalls who were made aware of the sub-lease and accepted rent from the husband. In March 1961 the freeholders granted a 99-year building lease of the property to T Ltd, subject to the wife's 1949 lease. Shortly after T Ltd sought possession from Critalls, who in turn served notice on the husband to determine the sub-lease. In September 1961 the husband allowed his stepdaughter to live in the premises rent-free. In March 1962 the lease was transferred to the plaintiffs who knew of the sub-lease. After various inconclusive dealings with the Land Registry, the plaintiffs sought a declaration that the sub-lease was void for lack of registration substantively or by entry against the superior lease. The first defendant claimed to be entitled to be registered as sub-leaseholder with priority over the plaintiff. He claimed in the alternative an overriding interest under section 70(1)(g).

HELD: (C.A.) The first defendant was entitled to entry of a notice of the sub-lease against the superior lease from the time of application not earlier. It therefore did not have priority. The second defendant, the stepdaughter, was in occupation on her own behalf as licensee not on behalf of the first defendant. As he was not in actual occupation or in occupation by virtue of the second defendant and he was not in receipt of rent he could not claim an overriding interest. [1965] Ch. 958.

COMMENTARY

This case is an example of failure to protect by a variety of methods. The sub-lease being over 21 years may have been substantively registrable. If could also have been entered against the superior lease as a caution or as a notice with the superior leaseholder's assent. If he had been in actual occupation or received rent from the step-daughter, he could have claimed an overriding interest as he did have a proprietary right upon which to base it. She could not claim an overriding interest because although she was in actual occupation she had no proprietary right being merely a licensee.

KEY PRINCIPLE: *Actual occupation may be actual or apparent occupation.*

Chhokar v. Chhokar 1984

A husband held the legal title on matrimonial home on trust for himself and his wife. He entered into an arrangement to secretly transfer the title to a friend at an undervalue. They arranged to complete the purchase whilst the wife was in hospital giving birth. The husband took the proceeds himself and left the country. When the wife returned from hospital she found the locks changed and was excluded from the property. The husband's friend put the house up for sale at market value. The wife claimed an overriding interest of actual occupation.

HELD: (C.A.) The wife was not literally in actual occupation at the time of the husband's friend becoming the proprietor. The continuing presence of her furniture with and her continuing intention to occupy was sufficient to constitute actual occupation for the purposes of section 70(1)(g) of the *Land Registration Act 1925* [1984] F.L.R. 313.

COMMENTARY
The facts of the case may have led the court to interpret actual occupation generously. In *Hodgson v. Marks* [1971] Ch. 892 the test was said to be more literal. There the fact of occupation was effective notwithstanding that the vendor registered proprietor was also in occupation. The onus is on the purchaser to enquire as to possible claimants to overriding interests. Whilst *Williams & Glyns Bank Ltd. v. Boland* suggests that the test is one of fact not law, the courts have not allowed claims based on short-term, (*Abbey National Building Society v. Cann* below), or transient presence, (*Lloyds Bank v. Rossett* [1991] 1 A.C. 107). In *Kling v. Keston Properties Ltd.* (1983) 49 P.&C.R. 212 the presence of the plaintiff's car was held to be sufficient actual occupation where the defendant maliciously blocked the plaintiff's car. In *Epps v. Esso Petroleum Co. Ltd.* [1973] W.L.R. 1081, below, it was held that parking at unknown times in an unidentified place did not amount to actual occupation.

KEY PRINCIPLE: *Actual occupation must exist at the time of the creation of the transferee's interest in order to override the transferee.*

Abbey National Building Society v. Cann 1991

The first defendant applied to the plaintiff for a loan to purchase a house on the basis that she would be sole occupier. He in fact intended to live there with his mother and her future husband, the second and third defendants. The plaintiff inspected the property and the loan was formally offered and accepted. Contracts were exchanged on July 19, 1984, the money was advanced on August 6, the mortgage was executed before August 13, completion took place on August 13. The first and third defendant arrived at 10 a.m. that morning and began moving their furniture in at 11.45 a.m. On September 13 the first defendant was registered as sole proprietor. The first defendant defaulted on the loan. The Building Society brought repossession proceedings. The second defendant claimed a beneficial interest by virtue of her contribution to the purchase of a previously shared home and an assurance by the first defendant that she would always have a roof over her head. She also claimed to have an overriding interest of actual occupation. At first instance it was inferred that the charge was completed at 9 a.m. so that the defendants were not in occupation at the time of completion. The Court of Appeal said completion took place at 12.20 p.m. but found that the second defendant impliedly authorised the first defendant to create a charge having priority over her interest.

HELD: (H.L.) Neither of these artifices was necessary. For the purposes of sections 20(1) and 23(1) the relevant date for determining the existence of overriding interests was the date of registration of the estate not transfer or creation. However, for the purposes of section 70(1)(g) the person claiming must have been in actual occupation at the time of creation or transfer of the legal estate. The transactions of acquiring the estate and granting the mortgage were indivisible. There was no scintilla of time from the acquisition of the estate to the grant of the mortgage in which the second defendant's actual occupation based on a claimed beneficial interest could fit to bind the mortgagee. Occupation from 11.45a.m. on the day till 12.20 p.m. could not make for an overriding interest. In any case the acts on the day were preparatory to moving in to reside and did not have a sufficient degree of permanence and continuity to constitute actual occupation. [1991] 1 A.C. 56.

COMMENTARY

In respect of actual occupation, the date of occupation has been moved back from registration of the transferee's (mortgagee's) interest to the creation of the interest. This closes the registration gap between creation and registration where another interest could be fitted. The date of registration remains the effective date for the transfer of interests to take effect in law for other purposes. The case also closes the gap between acquisition of an estate and grant of a mortgage. Logically one cannot grant something out of a property until it is owned. The court, however, recognised the reality that for practical purposes they are one transaction where the purchase is dependent upon a loan secured by the mortgage. This overruled *Church of England Building Society v. Piskor* [1954] Ch. 553.

KEY PRINCIPLE: *The postponement or waiver of an overriding interest against the a subsequent purchaser or transferee is only effective if expressed on the Register.*

Woolwich Building Society v. Dickman 1996

The defendant granted his parents in law a Rent Act protected tenancy of a flat. He later obtained a loan from the plaintiff on the security of the property. As the plaintiff treated the parents-in-law as having beneficial interest in the property, they were required to sign consent forms postponing whatever rights they had in the property to the plaintiff. When the plaintiff defaulted on his loan, the plaintiff sought possession of the property.

HELD: (C.A.) The parents-in-law' rights as Rent Act protected tenants could not be postponed or removed by the consent forms. The plaintiff would only be entitled to the possession of the property if the requirements of the *Rent Act 1977* had been satisfied. On the facts of the case, the requirements had not been satisfied. Further, in accordance with section 70(1) of the *Land Registration Act 1925*, the consent form signed by the parents-in law was ineffective to postpone overriding interests arising under section 70(1)(g) of the *Land Registration Act 1925*, unless the consent was expressed on the register. As the plaintiff failed to do this, the parents-in law' rights were binding on the plaintiff. [1996] 3 All E.R. 204.

COMMENTARY
The consent to postpone overriding rights as against the mortgagee or purchaser is ineffective if not entered on the register. This appears to be contrary to established authority where registration of the consent has always been regarded as unnecessary, although, strictly speaking this is referred to in the section itself.

Rectification and Indemnity

KEY PRINCIPLE: *The court has discretion to refuse rectification of the Register within its powers under section 82 of the Land Registration Act 1925.*

Epps v. Esso Petroleum Co. Ltd 1973

A property originally included a house and an adjacent commercial garage. The house was conveyed to E along with a 11-foot strip of frontage. E and her successors covenanted to build a wall to divide the house and garage but never did so. In 1955 the garage was leased to J for eight years; the lease purported to include the 11-foot frontage. In 1959 the freehold of the garage was conveyed to B subject to J's lease and repeating the error as to the frontage. B was registered as owner of the garage and frontage. This title was transfered to the defendants in 1964. In 1968 E conveyed the house to the plaintiff and the apparent double ownership of the frontage came to light. The plaintiffs sought rectification of the register and claimed actual occupation by virtue of J often having parked his car on the frontage. J was E's personal representative. The plaintiff's argument was that he used the parking space in that capacity rather than as lessee of the garage.

HELD: (Ch.D.) Parking the car for an unknown time on an unidentified space was not occupation and did not amount to actual occupation for the purposes of section 70(1)(g). There was no actual occupation at the time of the conveyance to the defendants. The defendants were in possession and the court refused to exercise its discretion to order rectification of the register to return the frontage to the plaintiffs. [1973] 1 W.L.R. 1071.

COMMENTARY
The grounds for rectification are set out in section 82 of the *Land Registration Act 1925*. This case did not fall within the

area of discretion to order rectification. There is a general power to order rectification where it is thought just and equitable to do so. In *Norwich Building Society v. Steed* [1992] 3 W.L.R. 669, the court refused rectification where the sale had been executed by a mother under her power of attorney granted by her son. The sale was fraudulently induced by the daughter. The mother had sufficient awareness of the effect of the transfer document and the son could not rely on her alleged ignorance, having originally granted the power of attorney to the mother. Section 82 sets out the grounds for rectification but does not specify the time from which rectification should take effect. In *Freer v. Unwins* [1976] Ch. 288 a restrictive covenant having previously been on the Land Charges Register did not appear on the Register because of some error when the land came into the registered system. The Register was rectified from the time of next publication and was not backdated to the time when a lease was granted over the land. The lessee thus took free of the covenant but subsequent dispositions would be subject to registration.

KEY PRINCIPLE: *A party suffering loss from an error in the Register is entitled to an indemnity from the Registry.*

Clark v. Chief Land Registrar 1994

Two judgement debtors were owners of land which was subject to a charge to a bank which was registered. The plaintiffs who were judgement creditors obtained a charging order *nisi* against the property which they entered as a caution in August 1990. The order was made absolute and a further caution was entered in November 1990. The second defendant advanced money to the judgement debtors secured by a charge on the land. This charge was presented for registration in December 1990. The Registry failed to give notice to the plaintiffs under section 55 of the *Land Registration Act 1925*; the creditors thus did not challenge the registration.. The charge thus took effect subject to the earlier charge to the bank but not to the plaintiffs' charges.

HELD: (C.A.) Sections 55 and 56 of the *Land Registration Act 1925* described the nature and effect of cautions. Lodging of a caution did not give priority to the interest upon which the caution was founded. The second defendant's charge which was registered later took priority over the plaintiff's charging orders. An error had been made by the Registrar. The plaintiffs were entitled to an indemnity under section 83 of the *Land Registration Act 1925*. [1994] Ch. 370.

COMMENTARY

The method of entering a caution is very commonly used by lenders. As can be seen from this case it is not an absolute form of protection. Firstly, the caution does not protect the underlying interest per se but should prevent dealings. Secondly, the Registrar may make an error by failing to notify the cautioner of dealings. The appeal of *Chancery Plc v. Ketteringham* [1993] T.L.R. 954 (above) was heard with this case and dismissed.

3. FORMAL AND INFORMAL METHODS OF ACQUISITION OF INTERESTS IN LAND

[A] CONTRACT AND CONVEYANCE

Contract for the sale of land

Introduction

Section 2 of the *Law of Property (Miscellaneous Provisions) Act 1989* provides that all contracts for the sale of land must be in writing, incorporate all the terms which the parties have agreed in one document (or where contracts are exchanged, in each of them), and signed by or on behalf of each party to the contract.

The section further provides that the terms of the contract may be incorporated in one document, either by being set out in the document itself, or, by reference to some other document.

KEY PRINCIPLE: *There must be an exchange of contracts or one document containing all the terms of the agreement between the parties.*

Commission for the New Towns v. Cooper (Great Britain) Ltd 1995

The issue arose as to whether correspondence between the parties could constitute an exchange of contracts for the purposes of section 2 of *Law of Property (Miscellaneous Provisions) Act 1989*.

HELD: (C.A.) Section 2 of the *Law of Property (Miscellaneous Provisions) Act 1989* could not be satisfied by an offer and acceptance contained in the correspondence between the parties. The court was of the view that section 2 required a greater degree of formality in contracts for the sale or other disposition of an interest in land. There must either be one document recording the agreement of both parties, or, a formal exchange of contracts incorporating all the terms of the agreement, with the intention that both parties be bound by the contract once the contracts are exchanged.[1995] 2 W.L.R. 677.

Hooper v. Sherman 1995

The Court was asked to consider whether a legally valid contract to transfer the plaintiff's share in the property and mortgage liability to the defendant had come into existence by an exchange of letters.

HELD: (C.A.) An exchange of letters was sufficient to form the written contract for the sale of land for the purposes of section 2 of the *Law of Property (Miscellaneous Provisions) Act 1989*. This was because the letters dealt with the essential terms of the contract and therefore amounted to an exchange of contracts which formed a valid agreement under section 2. The court also noted that the use of the word "without prejudice" did not prevent a contract from coming into existence. *Current Law Digest*, March 1995, at 20.

COMMENTARY

The two cases are clearly in conflict. Both cases can be supported in different ways. It may now be necessary for the House of Lords to clarify the position as to whether correspondence between the parties does satisfy the requirements of section 2 of the 1989 Act. It should also be noted that although the 1989 Act abolishes the doctrine of part performance in such contracts, it does not prevent the doctrine of estoppel from applying in cases where section 2 is not complied with but the requisite elements of estoppel are present.

KEY PRINCIPLE: *Section 2 of the* Law of Property (Miscellaneous Provisions) Act 1989 *only applies to executory and not executed contracts.*

Tootal Clothing Ltd v. Guinea Properties Ltd 1992

The plaintiff and the defendants signed two agreements. One of these was an agreement to grant a lease and the other was a supplemental agreement, wherein it was agreed that the defendant would contribute towards the costs of the plaintiff's shop fitting works. The defendant alleged that the supplemental agreement was invalid because of section 2 of the *Law of Property (Miscellaneous Provisions) Act 1989*.

HELD: (C.A.) Both the agreements were valid as section 2 only applied to executory and not executed contracts. The supplemental agreement was not a contract in respect of a disposition of an interest in land, and therefore, once the lease had been granted, section 2 was inapplicable. (1992) 64 P.&C.R. 452.

KEY PRINCIPLE: *The word "signed" in section 2 of the* Law of Property (Miscellaneous Provisions) Act 1989 *should be interpreted in its ordinary sense.*

First Post Homes Ltd v. Johnson 1995

In 1993, the vendor orally agreed to sell some land to the purchaser. The purchaser prepared a letter for the vendor to sign. This letter set out the purchaser's agreement to purchase the land and had typed the purchaser's name at the top of the letter. The purchaser did not sign the letter but signed the enclosed plan. The purchaser applied for specific performance of the contract, and the personal representatives of the vendor applied to strike out the purchaser's claim.

HELD: (C.A.) The purchaser's appeal would be dismissed as the letter and plan could not be regarded as a single document for the purposes of the 1989 Act. They were separate and distinct documents. Also, the typing of the purchaser's name at the top of the letter was not a signature within the meaning of section 2 of the Act. Accordingly, there was no complete contract.[1995] 4 All E.R. 355.

COMMENTARY
In the case, Peter Gibson L.J. suggested that the word "signed" in s.2 of the 1989 Act should be interpreted in plain modern English. He further suggested, that the earlier cases on the interpretation of what amounted to a signature for the purposes of the Statute of Frauds and section 40 of the *Law of Property Act 1925* should not apply to the interpretation of the same word in section 2.

KEY PRINCIPLE: *A lock-out agreement does not need to comply with section 2 of the* Law of Property (Miscellaneous Provisions) Act 1989.

Pitt v. PHH Asset Management Ltd 1993

The plaintiff made an offer to purchase the defendant's property. The defendant agreed with the plaintiff that it would not consider any further offers for the property, provided, contracts for the sale of the property were exchanged within two weeks. This was confirmed in writing by the plaintiff. The defendant sold the property to a third party during this period.

HELD: (C.A.) The lock-out agreement (by which the defendant agreed not to consider other offers during the operative period) was not one which need compliance with section 2 of the *Law of Property (Miscellaneous Provisions) Act 1989*. The defendant was in breach of this agreement.[1993] 1 W.L.R. 327.

COMMENTARY
The use of the lock-out agreement would prevent the practice of gazumping from taking place.

KEY PRINCIPLE: *Where a contract is contained in two parts, a court may hold that there are two separate contracts, one being the main contract which is subject to section 2 and the other, a collateral contract which is not.*

Record v. Bell 1991

The vendor and purchaser of a property signed a contract in two parts, subject to exchange of contracts. The vendor agreed to give a warranty with regards to the state of the title. This was for the purpose of inducing the purchaser to exchange contracts. Although the contracts were exchanged, the purchaser did not complete the purchase. The vendor applied for specific performance of the contract.

HELD: (Ch.D.) This contract was enforceable as it complied with section 2 of the 1989 Act. There were two separate contracts, one being the main agreement between the parties which complied with the statutory requirements and the other, the warranty, was a collateral contract which did not require compliance with section 2. [1991] 1 W.L.R. 853.

COMMENTARY
These cases seem to suggest that the courts appear to take a liberal approach in trying to save these agreements rather than invalidate them under section 2 of the *Law of Property (Miscellaneous Provisions) Act 1989*. Compare *Tootal Clothing Ltd v. Guinea Properties Ltd*, above.

KEY PRINCIPLE: *The variation of a material term in a contract for the sale or disposition of an interest in land has to comply with section 2 of the* Law of Property (Miscellaneous Provisions) Act 1989.

McCausland v. Duncan Lawrie Ltd 1996
Earlier court proceedings resulted in the court granting an order that the plaintiffs would purchase the property from the defendant for £210,000 with completion fixed on March 26, 1995. This settlement agreement was in compliance with section 2 of the 1989 Act. As the day fixed for completion was a Sunday, the defendants' solicitors wrote to the plaintiffs' solicitors suggesting March 24, 1995 as the completion date. The plaintiffs' solicitors agreed to it in writing. The plaintiffs were unable to complete and the defendants issued a completion notice for compliance in ten days. The defendants then issued a rescission notice on the expiry of the completion notice. The plaintiffs applied for specific performance of the compromised agreement and the question arose as to whether compliance with section 2 of the 1989 Act was necessary with respect to the variation of the contract.

HELD: (C.A.) That compliance with the formalities laid down in section 2 of the 1989 Act was necessary where there was a variation of a material term of the contract. The variation of the contract in the present case was material as it brought forward the completion date and therefore affected the time when either party may issue the notice to complete. The plaintiffs' appeal against the first instance decision would be allowed.[1996] E.G.C.S. 103.

COMMENTARY
It is therefore necessary for solicitors to consider carefully whether the term being varied is a material term. If it is then compliance with s.2 is necessary because, as was stated by the Court of Appeal, whenever the parties varied a material term, they were in effect entering into a new agreement and if s.2 is not complied with, the parties are relegated to their rights under the original contract.

KEY PRINCIPLE: *The grant of an option to purchase land has to fulfil the formalities laid down in section 2 of the* Law of Property (Miscellaneous Provisions) Act 1989 *although the exercise of the option did not have to.*

Spiro v. Glencrown Properties Ltd 1991
The defendant was granted an option to purchase land by the plaintiff. The defendant exercised the option by notice in writing within the stipulated time. However, the defendant failed to complete the purchase. The grant of the option had been signed by both the parties but only the defendant signed the notice exercising the option to purchase.

HELD: (Ch.D.) That for the purposes of section 2 of the 1989 Act, an option to purchase land should be regarded as being equivalent to a contract for the sale of land conditional on the purchaser's exercise of the option. The 1989 Act did not prevent the agreement creating or granting the option from being the relevant contract for the purposes of the Act. The grant of the option had to comply with section 2, which it did in this case. Thus, the option to purchase was valid. [1991] Ch. 537.

Armstrong & Holmes Ltd v. Holmes 1993
One of the issues in this case was whether the exercise of the option to purchase had to comply with section 2 of the 1989 Act.

HELD: (Ch.D.) The court applied *Spiro v. Glencrown Properties Ltd* (above) and decided that the exercise of the option to purchase land did not have to comply with section 2 of the 1989 Act, so long as the grant of the option had complied with these formalities.[1993] 1 W.L.R. 1482.

COMMENTARY
It is clear from these cases that the grant of an option to purchase land will have to comply with the formalities laid down in section 2 of the 1989 Act. The cases suggest that an option to purchase can be regarded as a conditional contract which therefore brings it within the ambit of the statutory provision.

Conveyance

In order for the title to the land to be validly transferred to the other party to the contract, the general rule applicable is as contained in section 52(1) of the *Law of Property Act 1925*. This provides that "[a]ll conveyances of land or of any interest therein are void for the purposes of conveying or creating a legal estate unless made by deed." There are a number of exceptions to this, the most notable being section 54 of the *Law of Property Act 1925*, which removes the need for a deed in the case of a grant of lease for less than three years. In the case of registered land, there is the additional requirement that the transfer must be completed by registration in the appropriate manner.

For the deed to be valid, it has to comply with the statutory requirements for a deed contained in section 1 of the *Law of Property (Miscellaneous Provisions) Act 1989*. Generally, the deed must be in writing, signed and delivered.

[B] ADVERSE POSSESSION

KEY PRINCIPLE: *Possession of land can only be adverse if it is shown that the trespasser is actually in possession of the land and there is intention to be in possession by excluding all others including the land owner from the land.*

Littledale v. Liverpool College 1900

The defendants owned two fields between which was a strip of land separated by hedges. This strip of land, which led from the highway to the plaintiffs' pasture, had been conveyed to the defendants with the fields. The plaintiffs had a right of way over the strip of land. More than twelve years before the commencement of the present action, the plaintiffs put up locked gates at each end of the strip. The plaintiffs commenced the action to restrain the defendants from trespassing on the strip of land.

HELD: (C.A.) The defendants had not been dispossessed of their rights to the strip of land because the act of the plaintiffs in putting up the locked gates may have been done with the intention of protecting their right of way against the public use of it. The plaintiffs had failed to demonstrate an occupation with the intention of excluding the owner as well as other people. [1900] 1 Ch. 19.

Powell v. Macfarlane 1977

In 1956, the plaintiff, who was aged 14 at the time, with the help of his friends went onto the disputed land, improved the fencing, cut the brambles and cut hay for the purpose of feeding the family cow. Thereafter he allowed the family cow to graze on the disputed land until it died in 1968. Between 1956 and 1973, the plaintiff went shooting on the disputed land from time to time. Subsequently, the plaintiff started business as a contractor to fell and treat trees and had put a sign on the disputed land in a manner which could be seen from the road. The plaintiff sought a declaration that he had been in adverse possession of the disputed land within the Limitation Acts for up to twelve years.

HELD: (Ch.D.) It was necessary in order to establish adverse possession, for the claimant to prove he had the requisite intention to possess and made such an intention clear to the world. On the facts of the case, the plaintiff's intentions at a time when he was aged 14, as interpreted primarily from his own acts, were to take various profits from the land and such acts were equivocal in the sense that they were not necessarily referable to an intention on his part to dispossess the owner of the land and to occupy the land as his own property. The plaintiff's claim therefore failed. (1979) 38 P. & C.R. 452.

COMMENTARY
Slade J. stated in *Powell v. MacFarlane* that the relevant principles relating to adverse possession were:

[a]   the owner of the land with paper title was deemed to be in possession and the law would, without any reluctance, ascribe possession to him or any other person claiming title through him, in the absence of contrary evidence;

[b]   a claimant to possession of the land without the paper title must show both a factual possession and the requisite intention to possess;

[c]   factual possession indicated a degree of appropriate physical control over the land which was dependent on the circumstances of the case, in particular the nature of the land and the manner in which the land of that nature was commonly used or enjoyed;

[d]   the requisite intention to possess involved the intention in the claimant's own name and on his own behalf to exclude the world at large, including the owner with the paper title so far as was reasonably practicable and so far as the processes of the law allowed. Such an intention must be made clear to the world at large.

The approach of Slade J. In *Powell v. MacFarlane*, has been followed in subsequent cases such as *Buckinghamshire County Council v. Moran* (below) and *Wilson v. Marton's Executors* [1993] 1 E.G.L.R. 178.

KEY PRINCIPLE: *The occupation or possession of land may be adverse even if the paper owner has no present use for the land but only a future intended use.*

Leigh v. Jack 1879

A piece of land, which was owned by Leigh was designated on the plans as being for an intended street which never materialised. Adjoining land was conveyed to Jack who operated a foundry on it and dumped materials used at his factory on this piece of land. This obstructed passage by carts on the piece of land but did not impede pedestrian access. In 1865, Jack enclosed an oblong portion on this piece of land and in 1872 he fenced in the ends of the intended street. An action was commenced in 1876 to recover possession of this piece of land.

HELD: (C.A.) The deposit of the materials by Jack on this piece of land was not adverse because as the owner had no present use of the land but to devote it for some future use, this was not inconsistent with the enjoyment of the owner.(1879) 5 Exch. Div. 264.

Buckinghamshire County Council v. Moran 1989

Buckinghamshire County Council were the owners of a plot of land. It was the council's intention that this plot of land be used for a future road diversion. Moran owned the adjoining plot of land. The Council did not fence the boundary between Moran's and its plot of land as a result of which Moran used the Council's land as part of his garden. Council employees who inspected the plot of land periodically noted that it was kept tidy. The plot of land owned by the council appeared as part of Moran's garden at all material times. Nine years after Moran started using the Council's land, the Council's solicitor wrote to him asserting the Council's title to it but no further action taken until a further nine years later when the Council commenced legal proceedings to recover possession of the plot of land.

HELD: (C.A.) An owner who retains land unused because he has a future intended use of land can be dispossessed. A claimant to a possessory title had to establish not only factual possession but also an intention to possess so as to amount to adverse possession. There was evidence in this case that Moran had acquired complete and exclusive control of the Council's plot of land and therefore his actions amounted to an unequivocal demonstration of his intention to possess the land. [1989] 3 W.L.R. 152.

COMMENTARY

In *Leigh v. Jack*, Bramwell L.J. stated that, ". . . acts must be done which are inconsistent with [the owner's] enjoyment of the soil for the purposes for which he intended to use it." The rule usually deduced from the case is that the occupation of the land by the trespasser is not necessarily adverse if the owner with the paper title has no present use of the land but only a future intended use. Thus, the occupation of the land by the trespasser at a time when the land owner has no present use of the land, means that such occupation is not inconsistent with the land owner's enjoyment of it.

This rule appears to be put in doubt by *Buckinghamshire County Council v. Moran*. This case suggests that the fact that the owner with the paper title has no present but merely a future intended use for the land does not automatically mean that occupation of the land by the trespasser can never be adverse. It is clear from this later decision that what amounts to adverse possession of the purposes of the Limitation Acts is ultimately a question of fact. The nature of the actions which can be regarded as evidence of adverse possession will depend on the character and nature of the land which is in dispute. There is an argument that after this decision, it may be easier for squatters to obtain title to abandoned property.

KEY PRINCIPLE: *Section 75* Land Registration Act 1925

(1) The Limitation Acts shall apply to registered land in the same manner and to the same extent as those Acts apply to land not registered, except that where, if the land were not registered, the estate of the person registered as proprietor would be extinguished, such estate shall not be extinguished but shall be deemed to be held by the proprietor for the time being in trust for the person who, by virtue of the said Acts, has acquired title against any proprietor, but without prejudice to the estates and interests of any other person interested in the land whose estate or interest is not extinguished by those Acts.

(2) Any person claiming to have acquired a title under the Limitation Acts to a registered estate in the land may apply to be registered as proprietor thereof.

Spectrum Investment Co. v. Holmes 1981

D was the registered assignee of the lessee of a 99-year lease granted in 1902. By 1968, H had acquired title to the land by adverse possession against D. H applied for and obtained registration as the proprietor of the leasehold with possessory title. The title under which D was registered as proprietor of the leasehold interest was then closed. In 1975 D purported to surrender her lease to S, who was the registered proprietor with absolute title to the freehold: S instituted legal proceedings against H, *inter alia* seeking an order for the deletion of H's title from the register or alternatively, rectification of the register by reinstating D as the proprietor of the leasehold.

Held: (Ch.D.) When D's title was closed, she was no longer able to surrender it as she had ceased to be the registered proprietor of the property. At that stage, the title to the property was vested in H and only H could surrender it. D was also not entitled to an order rectifying the register as the Registrar had registered H's interest in accordance with section 75(2) of the Land Registration Act 1925. [1981] 1 W.L.R. 221.

COMMENTARY

It is therefore clear that in the context of registered land, once the squatter acquires adverse possession of the land, the Registrar, if satisfied that the requirements in section 75 of the *Land Registration Act 1925* are satisfied, is under a duty to register the squatter with possessory title of the interest. In the case of a lease, the leaseholder's interest is extinguished and therefore is not in a position to surrender the lease back to the landlord. The position is different in the case of unregistered land. In *St Marylebone Property Co. v. Fairweather* [1963] A.C. 510, the House of Lords was of the view that a leaseholder who was dispossessed of his property could nonetheless surrender the lease to the lessor. The effect of which was to end the lease entitling the lessor to immediate possession of the land as against the squatter.

[C] PROPRIETARY ESTOPPEL

KEY PRINCIPLE: *For proprietary estoppel to be established, the modern position is that, it is necessary to show that the assertion of strict legal rights is unconscionable.*

Taylor Fashions Ltd v. Liverpool Victoria Trustees Co. Ltd; Old & Campbell Ltd v. Liverpool Victoria Friendly Society 1982

The second plaintiffs were the freehold owners of two properties known as No.21 and 22, Westover Road, Bournemouth. The title to the two properties were unregistered. The second plaintiffs granted to the predecessors in title of the first plaintiffs, a lease of 28 years of No.22 with an option to renew for a another 14 years if the lessees installed a lift in the premises. This option was not protected by registration as a Class c(iv) land charge under the *Land Charges Act 1925*. The second plaintiffs subsequently sold the freehold of No.21 and 22 to the defendants in 1949. At the same time, the second plaintiffs acquired a 42-year lease of No.21 subject to a break clause after 28 years if the lessees to No.22 did not exercise the option to renew.

The defendants were also the owner of the freehold of the adjoining No.20. In 1958 the lease to No.22 was assigned to the first plaintiffs, the latter installing a lift in accordance with the option, with the acquiescence of the defendants. In 1962, a 14-year lease of No.20 was granted to the second plaintiffs, also with an option to renew for a further period of 14 years should the lessees of No.22 exercise the option to renew that lease. Extensive work was done on Nos.20 and 21 by the second plaintiffs.

The first plaintiffs served a notice on the defendants in 1976 seeking to exercise the option to renew the lease to No.22. The defendants alleged that the option was void for non-registration and notice to quit was served on both the first and second plaintiffs. Both the first and second plaintiffs commenced an action seeking a declaration that the defendant were estopped from asserting their strict legal rights.

HELD: (Q.B.D.) The option to renew the lease in respect of No.22 was void against the defendants for want of registration as a land charge. Thus, the first plaintiffs were not entitled to exercise the option to renew. The fact that the defendants were not aware that the option was void at the time the lift was installed was one of the factors the court would take into account. There were other relevant factors present such as the fact that the defendants did not encourage the first plaintiffs in the belief that the option was valid, and also, that the first plaintiffs were unable to prove that the lift had been installed by them in the belief that the option was valid. With regard to the second plaintiffs, the defendants were estopped from exercising the break clauses in the leases. This was because the defendants had encouraged the second plaintiffs to incur expenditure in undertaking extensive work on the two properties in the belief that the option was valid. [1982] 1 Q.B. 133.

LIM Teng Huan v. ANG Swee Chuan 1992

The plaintiff and defendant purchased a piece of land jointly and transferred it into their fathers' names. In 1982 the defendant commenced construction of a house on the land. In 1985, the plaintiff and the defendant entered into an agreement where the plaintiff acknowledged that the construction was with his consent and agreed to give his half share in the land to the defendant in exchange for unspecified land, which the defendant expected to be allotted by the government. Upon completion of the construction of the house, the defendant went into occupation. The plaintiff, as administrator of his father's estate, commenced an action against the defendant claiming, *inter alia*, a declaration that he was entitled to a half share in the land. The defendant counterclaimed for a declaration that he was the sole beneficial owner of the land and for an injunction to restrain the plaintiff from entering the land or dealing with his share in it.

HELD: (P.C.) That even though the agreement in 1985 was unenforceable, it provided evidence of the parties' intentions and it could be inferred that the defendant completed the construction of the house in reliance on it. Although the plaintiff had not acted unconscionably in allowing the defendant to assume that he was the sole beneficial owner of the land on payment of compensation to the plaintiff, it would be unconscionable for the plaintiff to resile from that assumption. The plaintiff was therefore estopped from denying the defendant's title to the land, conditional upon payment of compensation. [1992] 1 W.L.R. 113.

COMMENTARY

This decision in *Taylor Fashions* is regarded as pivotal to the development of the doctrine of proprietary estoppel, albeit that it is only a first-instance decision. Prior to this decision, it was assumed that in order for proprietary estoppel to be established, it was necessary to satisfy the five probanda set out in *Wilmott v. Barber* (1880) 15 Ch. D. 96 (below). However, the *Wilmott v. Barber* probanda were unduly restrictive and did not apply to all different situations in which proprietary estoppel could arise. It applied to unilateral mistake cases (where one party has been mistaken as to his rights and the other party fails to take any action to rectify that mistaken belief). However, it did not apply to the imperfect gift (where a promise has been made to transfer the land from one party to another but the formalities have not been complied with) and common expectation cases (where both parties have dealt with the land giving rise to the expectation in one of the parties that he or she would have an interest in the land). Therefore, until the decision in *Taylor Fashions*, the development of the doctrine of estoppel was stifled. The requirement now is that it must be shown that it would be unconscionable to allow the enforcement of strict legal rights. Oliver J. stated that these types of cases, ". . . requires a very much broader approach which is directed rather at ascertaining whether, in particular individual circumstances, it would be unconscionable for a party to be permitted to deny that which, knowingly, or unknowingly, he has allowed or encouraged another to assume to his detriment . . . ." See also *Appleby v. Cowley*, *The Times*, April 14, 1982, and *Swallow Securities v. Isenberg* (1985) 274 E.G. 1028. However, it should be noted that the *Wilmott v. Barber* probanda would still apply to unilateral mistake cases. See *Matharu v. Matharu* (1994) 68 P.&C.R. 93 (below).

KEY PRINCIPLE: *In cases where proprietary estoppel involves the mistaken belief of the representee, the* Wilmott v. Barber *probanda may still be applicable.*

Wilmott v. Barber 1880

A lease in which Barber was the lessor and Wilmott the assignee thereof contained a covenant prohibiting the assignment of the lease without Barber's consent. However, both parties were unaware of this covenant and Barber upon discovering its existence, refused to grant consent to the assignment of the lease to Wilmott. Wilmott argued that Barber was estopped from asserting his strict legal rights because the latter had allowed the assignment without informing Wilmott of his mistake.

HELD: (Ch.D) Fry J. stated that a person would be deprived of his rights if "he has acted in such a way as would make it fraudulent for him to set up those rights." Fraud in this context required that five elements be proved. These are that (i) the claimant must have made some mistake as to his legal rights; (ii) the claimant must have expended some money or must have done some act on the faith of his mistaken belief; (iii) the owner of the land must have known of his own rights which are inconsistent with that of the claimant; (iv) the owner must have known of the claimant's mistaken belief; and (v) the owner must have encouraged the claimant in his expenditure of money or in other acts which he has done either directly or indirectly. On the facts of the case, it was clear that Barber was unaware of his rights and there was no evidence to suggest that he knew that Wilmott had been acting in ignorance of his own rights. As such, Barber could not be prevented from asserting his strict legal rights to refuse consent to the assignment of the lease. (1880) 15 Ch. 96.

Matharu v. Matharu 1994

The plaintiff was the owner of premises known as 223 Coventry Road, Ilford, which he acquired in 1968. This property subsequently became the matrimonial home to the defendant and the plaintiff's son. During the time when they stayed in the premises, the defendant's husband made extensive renovations to the premises. The defendant was under the mistaken belief that the premises belonged to the plaintiff's son. The marriage broke down in 1988 and two years later, the defendant obtained a court order excluding her husband from the premises. The husband died in 1991. The plaintiff emigrated to Canada later that year but returned a year later. The plaintiff applied for a possession order against the defendant. At first instance, the court found in the defendant's favour on the grounds that proprietary estoppel applied.

HELD: (C.A.) In order for proprietary estoppel to arise, the *Wilmott v. Barber* probanda had to be satisfied. On the facts of the case, the defendant had satisfied each of those requirements, and as such, gave rise to an equity which defeated the claim by the plaintiff for possession of the premises.(1994) 68 P.&C.R. 93.

COMMENTARY

Although the Court of Appeal in *Matharu v. Matharu* applied the *Wilmott v. Barber* probanda, the facts clearly demonstrate that it was a case concerning the unilateral mistake of one party giving rise to proprietary estoppel. As was suggested earlier on, the *Wilmott v. Barber* probanda are still applicable in this category of cases, although later cases such as *Swallow Securities v. Isenberg* (1985) 274 E.G. 1028, has suggested that the *Wilmott v. Barber* probanda are merely guidelines, albeit that they may nonetheless be "necessary and essential guidelines." In general, the overriding criteria for the application of proprietary estoppel is now one of unconscionability.

Assurance or Expectation

KEY PRINCIPLE: *Although the overall criteria for proprietary estoppel to arise is one of unconscionability, it is still necessary to satisfy three essential elements. The first essential element is that there has been an assurance or expectation given by one party to the other.*

Ramsden v. Dyson 1866

A yearly tenant undertook building works at the property subject to the tenancy in the belief that the landlord would eventually grant him a new lease of 60 years. Upon the landlord's refusal to grant the lease, the tenant commenced an action claiming to be entitled to such a lease.

HELD: (H.L.) On the facts of the case there was only a lease for year to year. Lord Cranworth LC stated that ". . . [i]f a stranger build on my land, supposing it to be his own, and I, knowing it to be mine, do not interfere, but leave him to go on, equity considers it to be dishonest in me to remain passive and afterwards to interfere and take profit. But if a stranger build knowingly upon my land, there is no principle in equity which prevents me from insisting on having back my land, with all the additional value which the occupier has . . . added to it." (1866) L.R. 1 H.L. 129.

Inwards v. Baker 1965

In 1932, a father encouraged his son to build a bungalow on the father's land, which the son did, and paid about half the cost. The bungalow was mostly built by the son. At the time of the father's death in 1951, the son was still living in the bungalow. He continued to live there until 1963 when the trustees of the land sued for possession, claiming that he was a licensee. Judgment was given in favour of the trustees and the son appealed.

HELD: (C.A.) The trustees would not be entitled to possession of the land. This was because the son had relied on the assurances by his father which had given rise to the expectation that he could live in the bungalow for the rest of his life. [1965] 2 Q.B. 29.

COMMENTARY
In order for the doctrine of proprietary estoppel to arise, it is
clear that three elements need to be satisfied. The first of
these elements is that there must have been an assurance
or representation made by the representor giving rise to an
expectation in the representee that some benefit would
accrue as a result of his detrimental reliance on the representation or assurance.

Reliance

KEY PRINCIPLE: *Secondly, it must be established that there
has been a reliance by one party upon the assurance given by
the other party.*

Pascoe v. Turner 1979
Turner moved into Pascoe's house originally as his housekeeper
but subsequently cohabited together. Pascoe had purchased the
house in which they were living in. Pascoe subsequently left
Turner for another woman but at the time had told her that the
property belonged to her. Turner stayed on in the house in
reliance of this assurance and spent money on repairs and
improvements to the property.

HELD: (C.A.) The doctrine of proprietary estoppel applied in
this case. This was because Turner had spent money on the
house, in reliance on the assurance given by Pascoe, that, the
house was hers. In the circumstances of the case, it was appropriate to order a transfer of the fee simple to Turner rather
than to merely give her a licence to remain in the house. This
was because a licence would not give her protection against a
purchaser with no notice and Pascoe's determined efforts to
evict her. [1979] 1 W.L.R. 431.

COMMENTARY
The question as to whether reliance can be established is a
question of fact dependent on the circumstances of the case.
It is necessary to establish that there has been reliance
because it is reliance which provides the causal link between
the assurance and the detriment thereby satisfying the overriding criteria of unconscionability. Thus for instance, in *Taylor
Fashions Ltd v. Victoria Trustees Co Ltd*, the first plaintiff
failed in their claim, *inter alia*, because they couldn't prove
that they had relied on the assurance by installing the lift. The

evidence was that they would have installed it even if they were aware that the option was void.

KEY PRINCIPLE: *The reliance can be inferred from the circumstances of case, where it can be shown that there has been an assurance made, and, there is conduct by the other party from which such an inference can be drawn.*

Greasley v. Cooke 1980

In 1938, Cooke was employed as a maid in Greasley's home. From 1948 she started cohabiting with one of Greasley's sons and lived with him until his death in 1971. Cooke received wages as a maid only until 1948 when Greasley died. After the latter's death, she continued living in the home performing the duties of a housekeeper for the rest of the family. After the death of the son with whom she was cohabiting, Cooke was served with a notice to quit. She refused to leave the home and possession proceedings were commenced against her. She alleged that the family were estopped from asserting their legal rights as the son with whom she had been living with and another of Greasley's sons had assured her that she could remain in the home for as long as she wished, rent-free.

HELD: (C.A.) That where assurances had been made, there is a rebuttable presumption that the claimant acted in reliance on those assurances and the burden of proof is on the person against whom the estoppel is sought to provide evidence to the contrary. This was satisfied in this case, which, therefore, gave rise to an equity in favour of the claimant. [1980] 1 W.L.R. 1306.

Wayling v. Jones 1993

Wayling and Jones lived together as a homosexual couple for 20 years and upon Jones's death, Wayling made a claim against the latter's estate. He alleged that Jones had promised him that he would be given the bulk of the Jones's estate upon the latter's death and that in reliance on this assurance, he provided domestic services for Jones.

HELD: (C.A.) That it was necessary to establish a link between the assurances and the detriment. However, it was only necessary to show that the assurances was an inducement for the other party's conduct not that it was the sole inducement. Once it was established that the assurances were made, reliance could be inferred, if, there was conduct from which such an inference could be drawn. On the facts of the case, proprietary estoppel applied as such an inference could be drawn. *Current Law Week*, 32/93, October 1, 1993.

KEY PRINCIPLE: *The doctrine of proprietary estoppel is not restricted to acts done in reliance on a belief relating to existing rights, but, can also be based on the belief that future rights would be granted.*

Re Basham 1986

From a young age, the plaintiff had helped out in her mother and stepfather's business, for which she was never paid but had understood that she would be entitled to her stepfather's property when he died. In 1947, the plaintiff's husband was considered moving to a job which entitled them to a tied cottage. However, the stepfather persuaded them not to, as he would help them acquire another suitable property. Subsequently, the stepfather purchased a tenanted property with money provided principally by the plaintiff's mother. The plaintiff's mother died in 1976 and her stepfather moved into this property which had been vacated by the tenants. The plaintiff lived near her stepfather. Both she and her husband helped the stepfather by looking after him, and doing various things around the property including laying the carpet and looking after the garden.

She was told by the stepfather that she would not lose anything by doing these things. A few days prior to his death, her stepfather indicated that he wanted to have a will made which would leave his money to the plaintiff's son and the plaintiff was to have the property. The stepfather died intestate.

HELD: (Ch.D.) The doctrine of proprietary estoppel also applied in cases where the acts of reliance on the assurance given by the representor was in the belief that future rights would be acquired. It was not limited to cases where the belief was that existing rights would be granted. On the facts of the case, as the plaintiff was able to establish that she had acted to her detriment in reliance on her belief, which was encouraged by her stepfather, that she would be entitled to his estate, she was absolutely and beneficially entitled to his estate, which included the house. [1986] 1 W.L.R. 1498.

COMMENTARY
Basham makes it clear that it is unnecessary to for the representee to have relied on belief that existing rights would be given but can be based on the belief that future rights would accrue. This approach has been followed in *Durant v. Heritage* [1994] E.G.C.S. 34.

Detriment

KEY PRINCIPLE: *The third essential element that needs to be satisfied in order for proprietary estoppel to arise is that the representee acted to his or her detriment in reliance on the assurance given by the representor.*

Dillwyn v. Llewelyn 1862
A father gave his son possession of a piece of land and signed a memorandum stating that the land was being given to his son as a gift. The attempted gift of the land to the son was invalid as the proper formalities for such transfer of land had not been complied with. The father consented and encouraged the son to build a house on the land at his own costs and expense. On the father's death, it was discovered that the father only left the son a life interest in the land.

HELD: (H.L.) The son was entitled to ask for a transfer of the fee simple of the land. This was because the son had acted in reliance on the representations made by the father to his detriment, by the expenditure incurred in building the house.(1862) 4 De. G.F. & J. 517.

COMMENTARY
It should be noted that the detrimental act or reliance can be the expenditure incurred by the claimant. However, it can include detriment other than expenditure. For example, in *Jones (A E) v. Jones (F W)* [1977] 2 All E.R. 231, the claimant had given up his home and his job and did various work on the property, in reliance on the assurance given by his father, and in *Greasley v. Cooke* (above), the detriment suffered involved the carrying on of housekeeping duties without any wages.

Remedies

KEY PRINCIPLE: *The Court has a discretion to grant the appropriate remedy, once it is satisfied that proprietary estoppel has been established. The modern approach is that the court will grant such remedy as will be necessary to enable the claimant to receive the minimum equity to satisfy the estoppel rather than to make good the expectation.*

Pascoe v. Turner 1979
(as above)

HELD: (C.A.) In deciding the appropriate remedy to grant, the court should grant the minimum equity in order to do justice to Turner. On the facts and circumstances of the case, it was appropriate to order a transfer of the fee simple estate in the house to her. Cumming Bruce L.J. stated that ". . . the equity to which the facts in this case give rise can only be satisfied by compelling the plaintiff to give effect to his promise and her expectations. He has so acted that he must now perfect the gift." [1979] 1 W.L.R. 431.

Matharu v. Matharu 1994
(as above)

HELD: (C.A.) On the facts of the case, the equity was satisfied by granting the defendant a licence to remain in the property for life or such other shorter period as she may decide. Roche L.J. decided that the defendant did not acquire a beneficial interest in the premises by virtue of the estoppel.(1994) 68 P.&C.R. 93.

Crabb v. Arun District Council 1976
Crabb negotiated with the Council for a right of way. No final agreement between the parties was reached. The Council fenced round its land with gates at appropriate points, one to allow for this right of way (point B) and the other to allow Crabb access over a right of way which he already had (point A). Before any agreement could be reached, and after Crabb had sold part of his land together with the right of access at point A, the Council removed the gate at point B and fenced the gap. The Council refused to grant an easement leaving Crabb with landlocked land. Crabb claimed that the Council

were estopped from denying him a right of access at point B and a right of way along the road leading to this point.

HELD: (C.A.) That it would be inequitable to refuse to grant Crabb an easement of way. The court was of the view that in deciding the appropriate remedy, it was unhindered in principle. However, there was a propensity to recognise the expenditure incurred by claimant or other detriment suffered rather than to make good the expectation encouraged. In this case, the equity could be satisfied by granting Crabb an easement without any payment to the Council. [1976] 1 Ch. 179.

COMMENTARY

The original approach of the courts, with respect to the appropriate remedy in any given case, was to grant such remedy which would realise the expectation of the claimant. The court adopted this approach in *Dillwyn v. Llewelyn* (1862) De. G.F. & J. 517, where the appropriate remedy to meet the expectation of the claimant, was to order a transfer of the property to the claimant. However, the modern approach to this issue is for the court to grant such remedy as would enable the claimant to receive the minimum equity to satisfy the estoppel. In *Pascoe v. Turner* (above) the court decided that the equity would be satisfied only with a transfer of the fee simple of the property. In contrast in *Matharu v. Matharu* (above), the appropriate remedy was to grant the claimant a licence to remain in the property for the rest of her life. In deciding the appropriate remedy to grant, it must be noted that the court can grant different types of remedies. Two of these remedies have just been discussed. The other types of remedies which the court can grant includes damages (*Baker v. Baker* [1993] 2 F.L.R. 247); the grant of a perpetual licence (*Plimmer v. Wellington Corporation* (1884) 9 App. Cas. 699; the grant of an easement (E.R. *Ives Investments Ltd v. High* [1967] 2 Q.B. 379 and *Crabb v. Arun District Council*) or the grant of a lease as seen in *Taylor Fashions Ltd v. Liverpool Victoria Trustees Ltd* (above). This list is not exhaustive but is intended to demonstrate the various remedies which the court can use in order to decide how the equity can be satisfied.

KEY PRINCIPLE: *In deciding what is necessary in order to satisfy the minimum equity, there is a need to maintain* *proportionality between the parties so that a just result can be reached.*

Sledmore v. Dalby 1996

The plaintiff and her husband bought a house jointly in 1962. In 1965, the defendant moved into the house when he married their daughter. Rent was paid until 1976 when the defendant's wife became ill and he became unemployed. The plaintiff's husband made representations to the defendant that the latter and his wife would be left the house on the death of the plaintiff and himself. Later, the plaintiff's husband transferred his share in the house to the plaintiff. The plaintiff's husband died in 1980 and the defendant's wife died in 1983. The defendant continued to live in the house rent-free. In 1990, the plaintiff gave the defendant notice to quit and possession proceedings were commenced. By that time the defendant lived there only two nights a week and was in employment. However, the defendant's daughter, who was 27, continued to live in the house.

HELD: (C.A.) That although an estoppel had arisen in the defendant's favour, the minimum necessary to do justice was to grant the order for possession taking into account the present circumstances of the case. (1996) 72 P. & C.R. 196.

COMMENTARY
Hobhouse L.J. stated that "it is always necessary to ask what is the assumption made by the party asserting the estoppel for which the party affected is to be treated as responsible. There is also the need for proportionality. The end result must be a just one, having regard to the assumptions made by the party asserting the estoppel and the detriment he has experienced . . . the effect of any equity had long since been exhausted and no injustice had been done to [the defendant]." It is therefore clear that the approach to be taken by the court in deciding the relevant remedy should include proportionality between the parties to the case.

4. CO-OWNERSHIP

Introduction

Until recently, whenever two or more persons acquired ownership of land, the *Law of Property Act 1925* automatically
imposed a trust for sale. This imposed an imperative obligation
on the legal owners to sell the property but with the power to
postpone such a sale. This has now been replaced by the trust
of land which gives the legal owners the power to sell the
property rather than an imperative obligation to do so. This
is as a result of the *Trusts of Land and Appointment of Trustees Act
1996*, which will be discussed in the next chapter.

In addition to the trust of land imposed by the *Trusts of Land and
Appointment of Trustees Act 1996*, there is the question of whether
the beneficial ownership is held by the beneficial co-owners as
joint tenants or tenants in common. It must be remembered
that the legal title is always held as a joint tenancy and can
never be severed: *Law of Property Act 1925* sections 1(6), 34, and
36(2).

Factors to be Taken Into Account When Deciding Whether the Co-owners are Beneficial Joint Tenants or Tenants in Common

KEY PRINCIPLE: *Co-owners who contributed to the purchase price in unequal shares are presumed to hold the
property as beneficial tenants in common.*

Bull v. Bull 1955

The plaintiff and his mother jointly purchased a house as a
home for the two of them. The property was conveyed into the
plaintiff's name as he had contributed a larger proportion of
the purchase price. The plaintiff subsequently got married and
differences occurred between the mother and the plaintiff's
wife. The plaintiff gave his mother notice to quit and applied
to court for possession of the house.

HELD: (C.A.) The plaintiff and the mother were equitable
tenants in common as they had contributed to the purchase
price in unequal shares. Both the parties were entitled to

possession .of the house and neither was entitled to evict the other. [1955] 1 Q.B. 234.

COMMENTARY
In the case of married couples, the court has sometimes reached the conclusion that the even though their contribution to the purchase price were unequal, a joint tenancy can be inferred. Further, it is presumed that mortgagees will hold the beneficial interest as tenants in common. In *Re Jackson* (1887) 34 Ch.D. 734, J, by his will, left all his real and personal estate to three sisters. His estate consisted mainly of land, the greater part of which was sold after his death. The proceeds of sale were used to invest on the security of mortgages of real estate with the three sisters being the mortgagees. They were described in the deeds as joint tenants. The court decided that notwithstanding the description of the mort- gagees as joint tenants, the mortgagees were in fact tenants in common.

KEY PRINCIPLE: *Business or commercial partners who pur- chase property or acquire a lease of business premises together are normally presumed to have purchased the prop- erty or acquired the lease as beneficial tenants in common.*

Lake v. Craddock 1732
Five individuals purchased some waterlogged land from the commissioners of sewers. The property was conveyed to them as legal joint tenants. They intended to drain the land and sell it for a profit.

HELD: The parties held the property as tenants in common in equity as they had contributed to the purchase price in unequal shares and the doctrine of survivorship was inconsistent with the commercial enterprise undertaken by the parties. (1732) 3 P. Wms. 158.

Malayan Credit Ltd v. Jack Chia-MPH Ltd 1986
The defendant had a tenancy of the seventh floor of a building which it occupied for its business purposes. It was agreed that the plaintiff and the defendant, which were separate companies and ran separate businesses, would share the premises and a lease would be granted to them both. The lessor granted a lease

of the seventh floor and car park spaces to the defendant and plaintiff as joint tenants at law. A dispute arose between the parties with regard to the area of occupation.

HELD: (P.C.) The situations in which equity would presume that joint tenants at law held the beneficial interest as tenants in common were not limited to cases of payment of purchase price in unequal shares, or the purchase of partnership property but included lessees taking a lease of business premises for their own separate purposes. On the facts of the case, an inference could be drawn that the plaintiff and defendant held the lease as beneficial tenants in common in unequal shares. Upon a sale of the lease, the proceeds would be divided in accordance with their respective shares.[1986] 1 A.C. 549.

COMMENTARY
These are some of the presumptions which equity would apply in deciding whether the co-owners, in the absence of any express agreement, held the beneficial title as beneficial joint tenants or tenants in common. However, these are only presumptions and like most presumptions they are rebuttable by evidence to the contrary.

Severance of the Beneficial Joint Tenancy

[a] Severance by notice in writing under section 36(2) of the Law of Property Act 1925

KEY PRINCIPLE: *The notice in writing for the purposes of section 36(2) of the* Law of Property Act 1925, *can be given by way of legal proceedings but must evince an intention to sever immediately.*

Harris v. Goddard 1983
Harris and his wife were joint tenants of their matrimonial home. In 1979 the marriage broke down irretrievably and Harris's wife petitioned for divorce. The petition contained a prayer for property adjustment orders. Harris was injured in a car accident three days before the hearing of the divorce petition and died about five weeks later. The plaintiffs who were the executors of Harris's estate sought a declaration claiming that the equitable joint tenancy between Harris and his wife had been severed prior to his death thereby creating an equitable tenancy in common in equal shares. The question arose as

to whether the prayer in the divorce petition amounted to notice in writing for the purposes of section 36(2) of the *Law of Property Act 1925*.

HELD: (C.A.) A notice in writing for the purposes of section 36(2) of the 1925 Act had to evince an intention to sever immediately. The prayer in the petition did no more than to ask the court to consider at some future time whether to exercise its jurisdiction under the *Matrimonial Causes Act 1973* and therefore was not sufficient to amount to a notice in writing of the intention to sever the equitable joint tenancy. The wife was therefore entitled to the whole of the proceeds of sale of the former matrimonial home.[1983] 1 W.L.R. 1203.

Re Draper's Conveyance 1969

The issue in this case was whether a summons (supported by an affidavit) issued by a wife under section 17 of the *Married Women's Property Act 1882* seeking an order for the sale of the matrimonial home and distribution of the proceeds of sale in accordance with the parties' respective interests, was effective to sever the equitable joint tenancy.

HELD: (Ch.D.) The wife's summons under section 17, together with her affidavit in support, showed an intention inconsistent with a continued equitable joint tenancy. The summons and affidavit was sufficient to amount to a notice in writing under section 36(2) of the *Law of Property Act 1925* to sever the equitable joint tenancy. [1969] 1 Ch. 486.

COMMENTARY

The effect of these cases is that the pleadings used in legal proceedings can, in some instances, amount to sufficient notice for the purposes of section 36(2) of the *Law of Property Act 1925*. The overriding criteria is that it must evince an intention to sever immediately. This intention was present in the summons and affidavit in *Re Draper's Conveyance*. However, it is not clear if the summons or the affidavit by itself would have been sufficient notice for the purposes of section 36(2).

Further, in *Re Draper's Conveyance*, Plowman J. accepted the argument of counsel for the plaintiff that the orders made under section 17 was not effective to sever the equitable joint tenancy. This was on the basis that the power of the court under section 17 of the 1882 Act was merely to declare the parties rights with respect to the property and not to alter those rights.

KEY PRINCIPLE: *The notice in writing should be served on all the joint tenants.*

Re 88 Berkeley Road, London NW9 1971

The plaintiff and the deceased were the joint tenants of a property. The deceased's solicitors sent a notice in writing to the plaintiff giving notice of the deceased's intention to sever the equitable joint tenancy. When the notice arrived at the property by recorded delivery, the plaintiff was not there and the deceased acknowledged receipt of the notice. Upon the deceased's death, the plaintiff claimed to be entitled to the property by reason of survivorship.

HELD: (Ch.D.) As the notice was validly served on the plaintiff in accordance with the *Law of Property Act 1925*, the equitable joint tenancy had been severed. [1971] 1 Ch. 648.

[b] Williams v. Hensman methods of severance

Section 36(2) of the *Law of Property Act 1925*, in addition to providing severance of the joint tenancy in equity by notice in writing, also allows the joint tenant to ". . . do such other acts or things as would, . . . have been effectual to sever the tenancy in equity." This refers to the methods of severance laid down in *Williams v. Hensman* (1861) 1 John & H. 546.

KEY PRINCIPLE: *An act of a joint tenant operating upon his own share may create a severance of that share. This would include an act of bankruptcy committed by the joint tenant.*

Re Dennis (A bankrupt) 1995

A husband and wife were the beneficial joint tenants of two properties. The husband committed an act of bankruptcy in September 1982. A bankruptcy petition was presented in December of that year. In February 1983, the wife died and in her will left her property to their two children. A receiving order was made in May 1983 and the husband was adjudicated a bankrupt in November 1983. The trustee in bankruptcy sought a declaration as to the beneficial ownership of the properties.

HELD: (C.A.) The title of the trustee in bankruptcy related back to the date of the husband's act of bankruptcy. The husband's act of bankruptcy in September 1982 severed the beneficial joint tenancy. The wife's half share in the properties therefore passed under the terms of her will. [1995] 3 W.L.R. 367.

COMMENTARY
There are various acts by the joint tenant acting on his or her own share which would sever the equitable joint tenancy. An act of bankruptcy is one of the ways in which this occurs. Other acts which would be sufficient to sever the beneficial joint tenancy include an alienation by a joint tenant of his beneficial interest to another either by sale, transfer or mortgage, entering into a specifically enforceable contract of sale (*Brown v. Raindle* (1796) 3 Ves. 257), and possibly the commencement of litigation (although there is some doubt as to this).

KEY PRINCIPLE: *A joint tenancy in equity may be severed by mutual agreement.*

Burgess v. Rawnsley 1975
In 1967, H and the defendant bought the house in which he was the tenant of the downstairs flat. The house was bought by them as joint tenants with them contributing equally to the purchase price. H bought the house with the intention of marrying the defendant but this intention was never communicated to the defendant. The defendant never moved into the house. There was evidence of an oral agreement between H and the defendant in 1968 where the defendant had agreed to sell her share of the house to H for £750. However, the defendant refused to sell her interest in the house. H died and the plaintiff, as administratrix of H's estate, claimed, *inter alia*, that there the joint tenancy had been severed in equity.

HELD: (C.A.) The beneficial joint tenancy had been severed in equity by virtue of the oral agreement in 1968 notwithstanding that the agreement was not specifically enforceable. [1975] 1 Ch. 429.

Gore and Snell v. Carpenter 1990
Mr Carpenter and his wife were the beneficial joint tenants of two properties. In 1985, MrCarpenter instructed his solicitor to

draw up a separation agreement. The draft agreement included a clause severing the joint tenancy of one of the properties. Mr Carpenter moved out of that property and moved into the other property. Subsequently they reached an agreement in principle regarding the transfer of the properties subject to an agreement relating to ancillary financial matters. A divorce petition was served at the end of 1986 but before the petition could be heard, Mr Carpenter died. The plaintiffs who were executors of Mr Carpenter's will sought declarations as to the beneficial ownership of the properties.

HELD: (Ch.D.) There was no mutual agreement between the parties that the beneficial joint tenancies for both the properties should be severed. Although an agreement in principle was reached this was subject to agreement regarding the ancillary financial matters which had not been reached. Further, the clause in the draft agreement severing the joint tenancy of one of the properties was ineffective as it was presented as part of the overall proposal which had not been accepted. The wife was therefore the sole beneficial owner of both the properties by operation of survivorship. [1990] 61 P. & C.R. 456.

COMMENTARY

The beneficial joint tenancy can be severed by mutual agreement even where there is no valid and enforceable agreement provided that there was in fact an agreement between the parties that severance should occur. In *Gore and Snell v. Carpenter*, the absence of an agreement as to all the terms enabled the court to reach the conclusion that there had been no severance of the beneficial joint tenancy. In contrast, in *Hunter v. Babbage* [1994] E.G.C.S. 8, a draft agreement relating to the sale and the division of the proceeds of sale between the parties who were beneficial joint tenants was drawn up but never signed. One of the parties died before the agreement could be executed. The court decided that there was severance of the joint tenancy in equity as the draft agreement was sufficient to serve as an indication of the common intention of the parties that the joint tenancy in equity should be severed.

KEY PRINCIPLE: *There may be severance by any course of dealing sufficient to intimate that the interests of the* *co-owners were mutually treated as constituting a tenancy in common.*

Gore and Snell v. Carpenter 1990

(as above)

HELD: (Ch.D.) On the facts of the case, there was no course of dealing between the parties whereby they had evinced an intention to regard the two properties as being held by them as beneficial tenants in common. In order for the course of dealing to be effective to sever the joint tenancy, there must be a common intention on the part of all the joint tenants to regard the joint tenancy in equity as having been severed, which was absent in this case.

COMMENTARY

Likewise, in *McDowell v. Hirschfield Lipson & Rumney and Smith* [1992] 2 F.L.R. 126, the facts of which were similar to *Gore*, the court decided that the negotiation and correspondence between the parties as to the sale of the former matrimonial home and the division of proceeds of sale, where no agreement was reached, was not a course of dealing in which both parties clearly evinced an intention that the joint tenancy should be severed. Ultimately it is a question of fact whether there is a common intention or agreement between the parties to treat the beneficial joint tenancy as having been severed. It should also be noted that a unilateral declaration of an intention to sever is ineffective to sever the joint tenancy: *Nielson-Jones v. Fedden* [1975] Ch. 222.

The three methods of severance considered here namely, the severance by an act of a joint tenant on his or her own share, mutual agreement and mutual conduct, are the methods of severance set out in *Williams v. Hensman*. Where the act by a joint tenant does not fall within section 36(2) of the *Law of Property Act 1925* or within the *Williams v. Hensman* methods, the joint tenancy is not severed in equity.

Liabilities Between Tenants in Common

[a] Rental obligations

KEY PRINCIPLE: *A rental obligation will be imposed on a co-owner who is in sole occupation of the co-owned property, where it is necessary to do equity between the parties.*

Chhokar v. Chhokar 1984

A husband (the first respondent) and wife (the appellant) were the beneficial owners of the matrimonial home. Although the house was in the sole name of the husband, the wife had contributed to its purchase and upkeep. The husband sold the matrimonial home, without the wife's knowledge, to the second respondent at an undervalue. Completion of the purchase was arranged at a time when the wife would be away at hospital giving birth. The husband then left the country and the second respondent tried to force the wife to leave the house by various means. As the wife had been in actual occupation for most of the time except for a short duration, she had an overriding interest in the house. At first instance, it was held that the second respondent held the house upon a trust for sale for himself and the wife in equal shares and ordered that wife should pay the second respondent an occupational rent. Further, the court ordered that the property be sold within nine months of the order. The wife appealed against the orders.

HELD: (C.A.) That in balancing the interests of the second respondent and the wife, and taking into account the fact that the second respondent had acquired the legal title to the house by a fraudulent conspiracy and his attempts to force her out of the house, no order of sale would be made. In the circumstances of the case, the wife's interest had to prevail over the second respondent. As regards the issue whether an occupational rent had to be paid by the wife, the relevant test as to whether such rent was payable was one of fairness. On the facts of the case, the second respondent stood in the shoes of the husband and as the wife had not sought to exclude the husband from the house, there was nothing to indicate that it would be fair to order the wife to pay an occupational rent to the second respondent.[1984] F.L.R. 313.

Re Pavlou 1993

The respondent husband and wife bought their matrimonial home in 1973. The house was transferred to them as beneficial joint tenants. The parties separated in 1983. The wife was left in sole occupation of the home, from which time she paid the mortgage instalments and costs of repairs and improvements to the house. In March 1987, a bankruptcy order was made against the husband with the result that the beneficial joint tenancy was severed. The house was thereafter held by them as beneficial tenants in common in equal shares. The husband's trustee in bankruptcy applied to the court for a declaration as to the beneficial interests in the house, an order for possession and an order for sale of the house. The wife agreed that the orders for possession and sale ought to be made but the wife alleged that she was entitled to be reimbursed in respect of her expenditure on the house.

HELD: (Ch.D.) The court would order the payment of an occupational rent not only in cases where one co-owner had ousted the other co-owner or co-owners, but in any case where it was necessary to do so in order to do equity between the parties. In the case of the matrimonial home, where one co-owner left the house as a result of the breakdown of the marriage, the co-owner who left would be regarded as having been excluded from the property. In this type of situation, an occupational rent would be payable. Where the tenant in common left the property voluntarily and would be welcomed back, it would not normally be fair in that type of situation to order payment of occupational rent. On the facts of the case, the wife would have to pay the husband an occupational rent from March 1986 onwards, when she presented her petition for divorce. From that date, it was clear that the husband would not be welcomed back to the matrimonial home. [1993] 1 W.L.R. 1046.

COMMENTARY

The overriding criteria as to whether occupational rent is payable between co-owners is one of fairness or where it is necessary to do equity between the parties. In *Re Pavlou* (above), the court was of the view that it would be appropriate to order payment of an occupational rent by the wife to the husband from the date when she presented her petition for divorce. This was because the court felt that the presentation of the divorce petition should be taken to constitute a refusal to take the other co-owner back into the house and a willingness to pay an occupational rent.

[b] Liability for repairs and improvements

KEY PRINCIPLE: *A co-owner who has incurred expenditure on repairs or improvements to the co-owned property cannot claim a contribution or repayment from the other co-owners, in* the absence of an express or implied agreement, or unless it was carried out pursuant to an obligation to a third party.

Leigh v. Dickeson 1884-85

The plaintiffs were trustees and part of the estate comprised of premises in Dover. The beneficiaries of the trust and the defendant were tenants in common of the property. They made a claim against the defendant for monies due as a result of the defendant's use and occupation of three quarters of premises in Dover. The defendant owned the other one quarter of the property. The defendant counterclaimed for monies which he had spent on repairs and improvements to the property.

HELD: (Q.B.D.) That no tenant in common was entitled to undertake improvements or repairs to the property and claim a contribution from the other co-owners, without any express or implied agreement of the other co-owners. The defendant's counterclaim would be dismissed. (1884-85) 15 Q.B.D. 60.

COMMENTARY

Lindley L.J. also suggested in that case, that there was no obligation on the other co-owners to contribute to the cost of repairs even though the repairs may be necessary and proper and the other co-owners receive a benefit from it.

KEY PRINCIPLE: *The co-owner who has incurred expenditure on repairs or improvements to the co-owned property has an "equity" which will allow him to make a claim against the proceeds of sale of the property where the value of the property has been increased as a result of the repairs or improvements.*

Leigh v. Dickeson 1884-1885

(as above)

HELD: (Q.B.D.) Cotton L.J. suggested *obiter*, that the co-owner who expended money on repairs or improvements to the co-owned property may be able to make a claim against the proceeds of sale where the value of the property has been increased because of the repairs and improvements.

COMMENTARY

Therefore, even though the co-owner may not be entitled to make a claim initially for a contribution towards the cost of repairs or improvements, a claim can be made against the proceeds of sale where the value of the property has been increased because of it. There are, however, practical difficulties with this principle, for example, where the property isn't sold until a long time afterwards or where the repairs or improvements does not increase the value of property.

KEY PRINCIPLE: *The quantum of the co-owner's claim against the proceeds of sale of the property, where the value of the property has been increased as a result of the repairs or improvements, will be on basis of either half the increase in value of the property or half of the actual expenditure, whichever is less.*

Re Pavlou 1993

(as above)

HELD: (Ch.D.) In deciding the quantum of a co-owner's claim in respect of expenditure incurred for repairs and improvements to the property, there was no difference in approach between beneficial joint tenants and beneficial tenants in common. The guiding principle was that a co-owner cannot take the benefit of an increase in the value of the property without giving an allowance for what had been spent by the other co-owner. In the present case, the wife would be entitled to the lesser of half the increase in value of the property or half of the expenditure incurred. [1993] 1 W.L.R. 1046.

COMMENTARY

Prior to *Re Pavlou*, there was some uncertainty as to whether the co-owner's claim against the proceeds of sale in respect of the increase in value of the property as a result of the repairs or improvement was on the basis of the proportionate share in the increase in value (see *Parker v. Trigg* (1884) W.N. 27) or on the amount of expenditure incurred (see *Re Jones* [1893] 2 Ch. 461). *Re Pavlou* decides that it is the lesser of a proportionate share in the increase in value or the expenditure.

[c] Occupation and use of co-owned property by a tenant in common

KEY PRINCIPLE: *No action in trespass will lie against a tenant in common merely because he has exclusive possession over a part of the co-owned property, provided that he does not occupy more than his just share and proportion.*

Jacobs v. Seward 1872

The plaintiff and defendant were assumed to be tenants in common of some lands at Ealing. The defendant entered into possession of the land, cut the grass, put a lock on the gate and carried away the grass for stacking as hay.

HELD: (H.L.) The circumstances in the case did not amount to ouster so as to enable the plaintiff to succeed in a claim for trespass against the defendant.(1872) L.R. 5 H.L. 464.

COMMENTARY

With respect to the use and occupation of the co-owned property, it is clear from this case that no action for trespass can lie against another co-owner merely because one co-owner had exclusive possession over part of the property. The only exception is where the use of occupation of the co-owned property effectively ousts the other co-owner or co-owners from occupying or using the property will an action lie for trespass.

[d] Rents from a stranger and profits from the land

KEY PRINCIPLE: *Where a tenant in common makes a profit from the co-owned land by his own efforts, by for example, cultivating the land, he does not need to account for this profit to the other co-owners. In the case of rents received from strangers, there is a duty to account only if the co-owner receives more than his just share and proportion of it.*

Henderson v. Eason 1851

Henderson and Eason were tenants in common of some properties in the County of Kent. Eason died in 1839. A claim for an account was made against Eason alleging that Eason, who had the care and management of these properties, had taken more than his just share and proportion of the rents and profits accruing from these properties.

HELD: (Exch) Eason would only be liable to account to Henderson if he had taken more than his just share and proportion of the rents received from strangers. However, where the profits accrued as a result of his own occupation of the land, by for example, his cultivation of the land, Eason was entitled to keep the all the profits. On the facts of the case, there was no evidence to indicate that Eason had in fact receive more than his just share.(1851) 17 Q.B. 710.

COMMENTARY
A distinction in this case is made between rents received from strangers and profits accruing to the co-owner because of his efforts on the land. The reason for this is that it was regarded as inappropriate that the co-owner who has done some work on the land, for example, by cultivating the land on his own, should have to share the fruits of his labour with the other co-owners. This is especially so if it is borne in mind that the co-owners would not have to bear a proportionate share of any loss suffered by the co-owner in the enterprise.

---

5. STRICT SETTLEMENTS AND TRUSTS OF LAND

Strict Settlements

Introduction

This is an area which has undergone recent statutory changes by virtue of the *Trusts of Land and Appointment of Trustees Act 1996* ("*TLATA 1996*"). This Act received its royal assent on 24th July 1996 and came into force on 1 January 1997.

Section 2(1) *TLATA 1996* provides that "no settlement created after the commencement of this Act is a settlement for the purposes of the Settled Land Act 1925; and no settlement shall be deemed to be made under that Act after that commencement." Therefore, after the commencement of the Act no strict settlement can created expressly or arise unintentionally. The *TLATA 1996* provides for the creation of the trust of land in its place. However, two exceptions are permitted under the Act;

firstly, where there is a resettlement of settlements in existence at the commencement of the Act and secondly, settlements created in the exercise of powers of appointment contained in settlements in existence at the commencement of the Act.

The law relating to strict settlements will be applicable to existing settlements but obviously its importance will diminish with time. A settlement will cease to be a settlement where there is no longer any land or heirlooms subject to it: section 2(4) of *TLATA 1996*.

The details of the trust of land will be considered in the next section. This is because the trust of land also replaces the trust for sale. In view of the significant changes in the law relating to strict settlements and its consequential diminishing importance, only a few of the more important key principles and cases will be considered.

Powers of the Tenant for Life

KEY PRINCIPLE: *The powers of the tenant for life cannot be restricted by the terms of the settlement.*

Re Acklom 1929
The terms of the settlement provided, *inter alia* that the trustees were to sell the house and distribute the proceeds to charitable organisations in the event that the tenant for life did not wish to reside or continue to reside there. The tenant for life lived in the house for a number of years before going abroad for health reasons. Due to illness her return was delayed and she sold the house in 1927 as tenant for life. The trustees sought a declaration as to whether the tenant for life had an interest in the proceeds of sale or the income arising from it.

HELD: (Ch.D.) The tenant for life had not forfeited her interest under the settlement and as tenant for life, she was entitled to the income from the proceeds of sale. Section 106 of the *Settled Land Act 1925* made it clear that any provision in the will or settlement which limited or prevented the tenant for life from exercising his or her power of sale was void. [1929] 1 Ch. 195.

COMMENTARY
This decision reiterates the point that once there is a settlement within the meaning of the *Settled Land Act 1925*, the

tenant for life's powers under the Act cannot be limited or restricted in any way. Any provision to the contrary would be void by virtue of section 106 of the Act. The courts had adopted this view even in respect to the predecessor to section 106. See *Re Ames* [1893] 2 Ch. 479. The section also makes it clear that it applies to settlements made before or after the commencement of the Act.

KEY PRINCIPLE: *"A tenant for life . . . shall, in exercising any powers under [the Settled Land Act 1925], have regard to the interests of all parties entitled under the settlement, and shall in relation to the exercise thereof by him, be deemed to be in the position and to have the duties and liabilities of a trustee for those parties."* Section 107 Settled Land Act 1925.

Hampden v. Earl of Buckinghamshire 1893

The tenant for life of settled land, part of which was mortgaged and part of which was not, proposed to raise a sum of money by mortgaging the whole estate in order to pay off the existing mortgages and some pecuniary legacies. The settlement provided for the payment of life annuities. The effect of the mortgage would deprive the annuitants of all benefit from the land. The result would be that it would benefit the remaindermen to the detriment of the annuitants.

HELD: (Ch.D.) The tenant for life would be restrained from effecting the proposed mortgage as he was not paying due regard to the interest of the annuitants.[1893] 2 Ch. 531.

Middlemas v. Stevens 1901

A settlement provided, *inter alia*, that the interest of the tenant for life, who was a widow, would cease upon her remarriage. The tenant for life purported to grant a lease to her fiancé, in the exercise of her powers.

HELD: (Ch.D.) The tenant for life would be restrained by injunction from granting the lease on proof that the sole purpose for it was to enable her to live in the property after her marriage. [1901] 1 Ch. 574.

COMMENTARY

By section 107 of the *Settled Land Act 1925*, the tenant for life, who has powers of disposition of the land, and is a trustee of the legal estate of the settled land, is required to have regard to the interests of the parties entitled under the settlement. Although the tenant may be legally acting within his powers, the court has the power to intervene in cases where the action or proposed action by the tenant for life fails to take into account the interests of all parties.

Dispositions of the Settled Land

KEY PRINCIPLE: *A purchaser dealing with the tenant for life in good faith shall not be bound by the terms of the trust and shall rely on the statements in the vesting deed.*

Weston v. Henshaw 1950

In 1921, a grandfather sold some land to his son who then subsequently sold it back in 1927. By his will, the grandfather settled the land upon his wife for life, then to his son for life and then to his grandson. The land was vested in the son in 1940 who then purported to mortgage it as the absolute beneficial owner. He was able to do this by suppressing all the documents relating to the settlement and the conveyance from himself to the grandfather in 1927, thereby giving the mortgagee the appearance that he was the absolute beneficial owner, by virtue of the conveyance of 1921. After the death of the son, the grandson sought a declaration as to whether the mortgage was good against him.

HELD: (Ch.D.) The mortgage was void in accordance with section 18 of the *Settled Land Act 1925*. The mortgagee could not rely on section 110 of the 1925 Act because the section only applied to purchasers who knew that they were dealing with the tenant for life. [1950] 1 Ch. 510.

Re Morgan's Lease 1972

In 1950, a tenant for life granted a ten-year lease of four rooms to the plaintiffs and another person. In 1960, upon the expiry of the lease, a document purporting to be a lease granted a term of the same property to the plaintiffs for another seven years. The lease contained an option to renew for another seven years on the same terms but without the option to renew. The tenant for life died in 1962. In 1967, the plaintiffs gave a notice in writing in accordance with the terms of the lease exercising the option to renew the lease. The new landlords of the property refused to comply with the notice.

HELD: (Ch.D.) The plaintiffs who had acted in good faith within the meaning of section 110 of the *Settled Land Act 1925*, were entitled to an order for specific performance of the terms of the contract. Section 110 was applicable whether or not the plaintiffs knew or did not know that they were dealing with a tenant for life provided they were acting in good faith. [1972] Ch. 1.

COMMENTARY

In *Re Morgan's Lease*, the court doubted whether *Weston v. Henshaw* was correct. The two decisions are clearly in conflict but the approach taken in *Re Morgan's Lease* is favoured by commentators such as Maudsley (36 M.L.R. 25 at p.28). The Court of Appeal in *Bevan v. Johnson* [1990] 2 E.G.L.R. 33 had the opportunity to examine this issue. However, the court failed to consider either of the two decisions and the effect of section 110 of the *Settled Land Act 1925*, although implicitly, the Court of Appeal seems to have followed the reasoning in *Weston v. Henshaw*. The issue remains unresolved.

Variation of the Settlement

KEY PRINCIPLE: *"Any transaction affecting or concerning the settled land, or any part thereof, . . . which in the opinion of the court would be for the benefit of settled land, or any part thereof, or the persons interested under the settlement, may, under an order of the court, be effected by the tenant for life, if it is one which could have been validly effected by an absolute owner." Section 64 of the* Settled Land Act 1925.

Hambro v. Duke of Marlborough 1994

In 1705, Queen Anne gave property to the first Duke of Marlborough. In 1706, an Act of Parliament was passed which provided that the titles of the first Duke and the estates should, in the event of the failure of his male issue, pass to his daughters and their male issue in tail male severally in succession with remainders over and that neither the first duke nor any other person "to whom the premises shall come or descend . . . shall have any power . . . to hinder, bar or disinherit any person . . . to or upon whom the . . . premises are hereby invested or limited, from holding or enjoying the same . . ." The first defendant was the tenant in tail in possession with the powers of a tenant for life. The second defendant was the first defendant's son and the tenant in tail in remainder who was considered to be incapable of managing the estates properly. The plaintiffs, who were the trustees of the settlement, sought the court's approval, under section 64 of the *Settled Land Act 1925*, for a scheme under which the first defendant was to execute a conveyance of the estates to the trustees of a new trust to be held on a trust for sale , upon trust to pay the income from the estates to the first defendant for life and subject thereto, on a protective trust for the second defendant and thereafter upon the trusts of the existing parliamentary settlement.

HELD: (Ch.D.) The conveyance by the first defendant was a transaction within the meaning of ssection 64 of the 1925 Act. Under that statutory provision, the court had jurisdiction to authorise the first defendant to execute the conveyance without the consent of the second defendant, even though it varied the beneficial interest under the Act of 1706. [1994] Ch. 158.

COMMENTARY

This case illustrates the contemporary approach of the courts with regard to the interpretation of the word "transaction" within section 64 of the *Settled Land Act 1925*.

Trusts of Land

Introduction

As noted in the previous section, the *TLATA 1996* abolishes current dual system of strict settlements and trusts for sale. It replaces them with the trust of land. One of the important distinctions between the two is that in the case of the trust for sale the trustees for sale have a mandatory obligation to sell with the power to postpone sale, whilst, in the case of the trust of land, the trustees of the land have the power to sell and the power to postpone sale.The important statutory provisions in relation to the trusts of land are as follows:

Section 3 *TLATA 1996*: This abolishes the doctrine of conversion in relation to land held by trustees subject to a trust for sale and vice versa, whether the trust was created or arising after or before the commencement of the Act. The only exception is where a trust is created by will and the testator died before the coming into force of the Act.

Sections 4 and 5 *TLATA 1996*: This converts a trust for sale, whether created expressly or impliedly, into a trust of land. This is done by way of amendment to the statutory provisions in relation to statutory trusts for sale (schedule 2) and by giving the trustees the power to postpone sale indefinitely notwithstanding any provision in the trust deed to the contrary.

Section 6(1) and (2) *TLATA 1996*: The trustees of the land are given all the powers of an absolute owner including the power to sell and lease the land which is subject to the trust. They can also convey the land subject to the trust to the beneficiaries where each of the beneficiaries is a person of full age and capacity who is absolutely entitled to the land.

Section 6(3) *TLATA 1996*: The trustees are given the power to purchase any land in England and Wales.

Section 6(5) *TLATA 1996*: The trustees are directed to have regard to the rights of the beneficiaries when exercising any of their powers under the section.

Section 7 *TLATA 1996*: The trustees have the power to partition the land or any part of it where the beneficiaries are of full age and are absolutely entitled to undivided shares in the land.

Section 8(1) *TLATA 1996*: The trustees' powers conferred by sections 6 and 7 can, however, be expressly excluded.

Section 9(1) *TLATA 1996*: The trustees of land are given the power to delegate, by power of attorney, any of their functions as trustees which relate to the land to any beneficiary or beneficiaries of full age and beneficially entitled in possession in land.

Section 10 *TLATA 1996*: A purchaser will not be concerned with the consent of more than two persons if the consent of more than two are required. Where consent of a beneficiary who is a minor is required, the consent of a parent who has parental responsibility for the minor will suffice.

Section 11 *TLATA 1996*: The trustees of land, shall, in the exercise of any of their functions relating to the land subject to the trust, as far as is practicable, consult the beneficiaries of full age and so far as is consistent with the general interest of the trust, give effect to the wishes of those beneficiaries. In the case of a dispute between the beneficiaries, the trustees should give effect to the wishes of the majority in accordance to the value of their combined interests. This is subject to the exceptions contained in subsection 2.

Section 12(1) *TLATA 1996*: A beneficiary who is beneficially entitled to an interest in possession in land subject to the trust, is entitled by reason of his interest, to occupy the land at any time. This is subject to the proviso, either, that the purposes of the trust included making the land available for the beneficiary's occupation or the land held by the trustees is available for such occupation.

Overreaching

The *TLATA 1996* retains the mechanism of overreaching for trusts of land by way of amendment to sections 2 and 27 of the *Law of Property Act 1925*. As long as the purchaser pays the purchase price to two trustees, the interest of the beneficiaries will be overreached. Where the trustees have delegated their powers to the beneficiary or beneficiaries by way of a power of attorney under section 9, the beneficiary or beneficiaries have the power to dispose of the property but cannot give a valid receipt to the purchaser. The proceeds of sale has to be paid to two trustees or to a trust corporation.

Further, section 16 (1) *TLATA 1996* ensures that a purchaser would get good title to the land even thought the trustees have failed to consult or have regard to the rights of the beneficiaries, provided that he complies with the overreaching mechanism. Section 16(2) goes on to provide that where trustees of land conveys land in contravention of section 6(6) or (8) and the purchaser has no actual notice of the contravention, the contravention does not invalidate the conveyance. The section does not apply to registered land.

Consent

KEY PRINCIPLE: *The exercise of the trustees powers can be made subject to a person's consent.*

Re Inns 1947

A testator died in 1945 and left a relatively large estate. He settled some money upon trust to pay the income to his widow until remarriage or during her life. He also devised a large house upon trust for sale. If the house remained unsold, the widow was entitled to live there. Thereafter, it was to be given to a local authority upon a charitable trust to use it for a hospital, with a provision that there should be no sale during the widow's life without the consent of the widow and the local authority. The widow applied for maintenance out of the income from the estate claiming that the testator intended her to reside in the house but that the income which she received from the will was insufficient to enable her to do so.

HELD: (Ch.D.) In the circumstances of the case, having regard to both the testator's and the widow's wealth, the income from the will was reasonable and sufficient. Her application failed. [1947] 1 Ch. 576.

COMMENTARY

The judge assumed that this device valid. The case did not address the question whether the local authority would have been entitled to the land if the court exercised its statutory powers to dispense with the consent of the local authority. In order to deal with the situation arising in *Re Inns*, section 14 of the *TLATA 1996* (below) provides that any trustee or person who has an interest in the land may make an application to the court for an order under the section. The section goes on to stipulate that the court may make an order relieving the trustees of any obligation to obtain the consent of or consult with any person in connection with the exercise of any of their functions. As such, any requirement of consent to the sale of the property may be waived by the court in the exercise of their discretion.

Court's Powers Under Section 14 *TLATA 1996*

The court has a discretionary power to make various orders under section 14 of the 1996 Act on the application of a trustee or any person who has an interest in property subject to a trust of land. Apart from making an order relieving the trustees from the obligation to obtain the consent of any person in connection with the exercise of *any* of their powers, the court may make any order relating to the exercise by the trustees of any of their functions or declaring the nature or extent of a person's interest in property subject to a trust. It gives the court broader powers than its predecessor, section 30 of the *Law of Property Act 1925* (which gave the court the discretion whether to order the sale of the property) . The latter is repealed by the *TLATA 1996*. Section 14 *TLATA 1996* gives the court the power to make an order declaring the extent of a person's interest in property subject to a trust and can also prevent the trustees from disposing or otherwise dealing with the property including the exercise or the prevention of the exercise of the trustees' powers.

In exercising its discretion, the court is directed by section 15 of the *TLATA 1996* to have regard to the intentions of the person or persons (if any) who created the trust (section 15(1)(a)); the purposes for which the property subject to the trust is held (section 15(1)(b)); the welfare of any minor who occupies or might reasonably be expected to occupy any land subject to the trust as his home (section 15(1)(c)); and the interests of any secured creditor of any beneficiary (section 15(1)(d)).

It remains to be seen how the court will exercise its discretion under ssection 14, but the court is directed by ssection 15 to have regard to the various matters contained in section 15(1). It is likely that the court will still have regard to the cases on section 30 of the *Law of Property Act 1925*. However, it should be borne in mind that, in some instances, the court, when faced with a similar set of facts, may reach a different conclusion on the basis that there is no longer any imperative obligation on the trustees to sell the property. The Law Commission in its report stated that "[t]he courts will not be required to give preference to sale, and in making orders, will not be restricted to making ones which are simply ancillary to sale."

KEY PRINCIPLE: *Where the purpose of the trust is still continuing, the court will be reluctant to order a sale of the property.*

Re Buchanan-Wollaston's Conveyance 1939

Four individuals who owned properties near or adjoining each other, combined and purchased a piece of land for the purpose of keeping it as open land so as to maintain their sea views. It was agreed that any transaction in relation to the land must be with the majority agreement of the parties. The plaintiff sold his property and wished to sell the co-owned land and divide the proceeds of sale.

HELD: (C.A.) As the collateral purpose (the primary purpose being the trust for sale) of the acquisition of the co-owned land (the maintenance of the sea views) was still continuing and subsisting, no order of sale would be made. [1939] 1 Ch. 738.

Barclays Bank v. Hendricks 1995

A wife appealed against the grant of an order, obtained by a creditor, for the sale of the matrimonial home under section 30 of the *Law of Property Act 1925*. The husband had already moved out of the matrimonial home and had moved into another property belonging to the wife. She argued that the sale of the property should be deferred until the children had reached the age of 18 or had finished full time education and that she did not want to move to the other property.

HELD: That the collateral purpose of joint occupation of the property as a matrimonial home had ended when the husband moved out of the home. As the wife had failed to show any exceptional circumstances why her interest should prevail against the creditor, especially since she had another property in the area, the order made under section 30 would be upheld. *The Independent*, November, 10, 1995.

COMMENTARY

In light of the *TLATA 1996*, it is submitted that the collateral (or primary) purpose will be one of the more important factors which the court will have to take into account when deciding whether to exercise its jurisdiction under section 14. The court is in fact directed by section 15 to take this factor into account when considering an application made under section 14. It should be noted that the reference to the term collateral purpose in these cases was because the trust for sale was applicable and as such the primary purpose had to be the sale of the property with any other purpose being merely a collateral purpose.

———————————

KEY PRINCIPLE: *Where the purpose for the acquisition of the property, which is subject to the trust, is for the provision of a matrimonial or family home and the marriage irretrievably breaks down, an application should be made under the Matrimonial Causes legislation.*

Jones v. Challenger 1961

A husband and wife bought a house as their matrimonial home as joint tenants. A short while later, the wife left the matrimonial home and the husband divorced her on the grounds of adultery. The ex-wife applied for an order for the sale of the house under section 30 of the *Law of Property Act 1925*.

HELD: (C.A.) An order for the sale of the property would be made. Where the circumstances show the existence of a purpose other than sale, the court would not allow the letter of the trust (for sale) to prevail. However, since the collateral purpose, namely the provision of a matrimonial home, was at an end, it would be appropriate to allow the parties to realise their investments.[1961] Q.B. 176.

Williams (J W) v. Williams (M A) 1976

A husband and wife bought a house in their joint names in 1970. In 1971 the parties were divorced on the basis of the wife's allegation of cruelty. The wife and their four children remained in the house with the wife paying the mortgage instalments and rates. In 1973, the husband applied for an order for sale of the house under section 30 of the *Law of Property Act 1925*.

HELD: (C.A.) Since the main reason for the acquisition of the house was for the provision of a home for the family and that purpose was still continuing, the husband's application should have been made to the Family Division under the *Matrimonial Proceedings and Property Act 1970* and the *Matrimonial Causes Act 1973*. Accordingly, the order for sale granted at first instance would be set aside.[1976] 1 Ch. 278.

COMMENTARY

Where the collateral purpose (which will now be the primary purpose) relates to the provision of a family home and even though the parties may have separated or divorced, so long as that purpose is continuing, it would be inappropriate to apply for an order for sale under the *TLATA 1996*. *Williams v. Williams* has made it clear that it would be more appropriate to use the court's powers under the Matrimonial Causes legislation. It is submitted that notwithstanding the *TLATA 1996*, this should still be the approach taken by the court. However, the *TLATA 1996* would be applicable in cases where the parties are not married and the property in question is the family home. See *Re Evers* [1980] 1 W.L.R. 1327.

KEY PRINCIPLE: *The primary purpose to the trust cannot be overridden by passing the beneficial interest of one party to another who was kept out of enjoyment of the property.*

Abbey National plc v. Moss 1994

M was the owner of a house which was occupied by herself, her daughter, her son-in-law and their children. She was persuaded by her daughter to transfer the house into their joint names. The daughter forged M's signature and obtained a mortgage from the plaintiffs. The daughter and her family subsequently left the country. The plaintiffs applied for an order for sale under section 30 of the Law of Property Act 1925 upon default of the mortgage payments.

HELD: (C.A.) The intention of the transfer of the house into the joint names of the daughter and M was on the basis that it would provide a home for M for the rest of her life. That purpose was still continuing and therefore taking that and the method in which the daughter acquired the mortgage into account, it was inappropriate to grant an order for sale. (1994) H.L.R. 249.

KEY PRINCIPLE: *Instead of making an order for the sale of the property subject to the trust, it may be appropriate to order payment of compensation by one co owner to the other.*

Dennis v. Macdonald 1982

In 1970, the plaintiff and defendant bought a house as their family home, with each contributing equally towards the purchase price part of which consisted of a mortgage. The house was conveyed into their names as tenants in common in equal shares. In 1974, the plaintiff left the house taking their five children with her. The defendant remained in occupation and later that year three of the older children returned to live with him. Mortgage payments were made by the defendant and the mortgage loan was fully repaid by March 1980. The plaintiff applied under section 30 of the *Law of Property Act 1925* for an order for sale of the house. At first instance it was decided that where the home was still needed in order to provide a home for the family, it was inappropriate to grant an order for sale of the property under section 30 of the 1925 Act. That as the actions of the defendant amounted to an ouster, the plaintiff, as a tenant in common, was entitled to occupational rent. The defendant appealed and the plaintiff cross appealed against these orders.

HELD: (C.A.) A tenant in common who had been excluded from occupation of the property was entitled to compensation. Since the defendant occupied the property by virtue of his beneficial interest, the proper way to assess the occupational rent payable was that the defendant ought to pay the plaintiff one half of such sum as would be regarded as fair rent under the *Rent Act 1977*.[1982] 1 All E.R. 590.

COMMENTARY

Where the court reaches the conclusion that an order for sale is inappropriate, and one co-owner is in occupation whilst the other is not, the court may in some instances order that the co-owner in occupation pays occupational rent to the other. Although the case was decided in the context of section 30 of the *Law of Property Act 1925*, the position is likely to be the same under the *TLATA 1996*.

The Trustee in Bankruptcy and the Trust of Land

KEY PRINCIPLE: *Where a spouse having a beneficial interest in the property becomes bankrupt, the interests of the creditors usually prevail over the interests of the other spouse, in the absence of exceptional circumstances, in* *relation to the question as to whether an order for possession and sale of the property ought to be made.*

Re Citro (A Bankrupt) 1991

In 1985 two brothers were adjudicated bankrupt. They both had a half share beneficial interests in their respective matrimonial homes. The trustee in bankruptcy of their joint and separate estates applied to the court for a declaration as to their respective beneficial share in the matrimonial homes and orders for possession and sale of the homes under section 30 of the *Law of Property Act 1925*. The judge at first instance granted orders for possession and sale but postponed them until the youngest child in each case turned 16 years of age.

HELD: (C.A.) That the orders for possession and sale would be postponed only for six months. Unless there were exceptional circumstances, which were more than the ordinary consequences of debt and improvidence, the interests of the children and their spouse could not prevail over the interests of the creditors. On the facts of the case, although the circumstances of their spouses and children were distressing, they could not be described as exceptional, therefore there was no justification for a substantial postponement of the orders for possession and sale. [1991] Ch. 142.

COMMENTARY

In the earlier case of *Re Holliday* [1981] Ch. 405, the Court of Appeal granted an order for the sale of the family home under section 30 of the *Law of Property Act 1925*, on the application of the trustee in bankruptcy, but postponed it until the second child of the family reached the age of 17. The postponement was substantial in that case. In *Re Citro*, the Court of Appeal regarded *Re Holliday* as an exceptional case with one special feature, in that, the postponement of the order for sale would not have caused any great hardship to the creditors. The Court of Appeal also stated that the series of bankruptcy decisions, including cases such as *Re Densham* (*A Bankrupt*) [1975] 1 W.L.R. 1519 and *Re Bailey* (*A Bankrupt*) (No. 25 of 1975) [1977] 1 W.L.R. 278, have usually held that the interests of the creditors would prevail against the spouse and the children and that a sale within a relatively short period of time would be ordered.

6. LEASES

Essential Elements of Leases

KEY PRINCIPLE: *A valid leasehold must be for a certain duration.*

Prudential Assurance Co. Ltd. v. London Residuary Body 1992

In 1930 a strip of land adjacent to a road was sold to the council and then leased back "until the . . . land is required by the council for the purposes of the widening of . . ." the road. The successors to the council who had no interest in widening the road sold the land to the other defendants. They in turn issued a notice determining the lease. The plaintiffs who were assignees of the lease sought a declaration that the lease could only be determined upon the land being required for road widening.

HELD: (H.L.) A lease has to be of a certain duration. The original agreement was for an uncertain period and was thus void. The land was, however, held on a yearly tenancy by virtue of possession and payment of rent. Service of six months' notice was sufficient to determine a yearly tenancy. [1992] 2 A.C. 386.

COMMENTARY

This confirms the principle in *Lace v. Chantler* [1944] K.B. 368 where it was held that an agreement for a lease for the duration of the war was uncertain and did not create a good leasehold interest. It overrules *Ashburn Anstalt v. W J Arnold & Co* [1989] Ch. 1 which seemed to go away from the principle in *Lace v. Chantler* in recognising a lease that was for indefinite duration could be regarded as certain because both parties had the power to end it. It also overrules *Re Midland Railway Co.'s Agreement* [1971] Ch. 725 in the sense that all leases must comply with the certainty rule and periodic leases are not exempt from the rule. It does not deny though that a periodic lease is of a certain duration if each period and consequently each period of determination is certain. In *Re Midland Railway Co.'s Agreement* a term allowing for determination of the lease when the lessors required the land for their undertaking did not void the lease as it was not inconsistent with the existing periodic lease.

KEY PRINCIPLE: *A valid leasehold must confer on the lessee exclusive possession of the property.*

Street v. Mountford 1985

An agreement granted the right to occupy two rooms subject to 14 days' notice to quit. It was titled a "licence agreement". The occupant signed a declaration to the effect that she understood that the agreement did not create a lease protected by the Rent Acts. Thereafter she and her husband moved in. A declaration was sought as to whether the agreement was a lease or a licence.

HELD: (H.L.) There was a grant of a term at a rent with exclusive possession. There was therefore a valid lease. Calling the agreement a licence was immaterial if there was in fact exclusive possession. [1985] A.C. 809.

COMMENTARY
The decision was important in restraining landlords from seeking to avoid the protection granted to lessees by the Rent Acts. The case disapproved *Somma v. Hazelhurst* [1978] 1 W.L.R. 1014 where emphasis was given to the stated intention of the parties. There two separate agreements were made with a couple to occupy a bedsit with a reservation that the landlord or nominee could also move in. Despite the unlikely match between the agreement and the reality the court held there to be no lease. Since *Street v. Mountford*, courts have been more astute to identify sham terms which neither party intend to rely on and should thus be ignored in determining whether factual exclusive possession has been granted. *A G Securities v. Vaughan,* and *Antoniades v. Villiers* [1990] 1 A.C. 417 are good examples of the application of the principle. The two actions were heard together. In *A G Securities v. Vaughan* four separate agreements were made at different times with different occupants to share a house. There was no joint tenancy with collective exclusive possession as they had different agreements on different terms. There was also no individual exclusive possession of identified rooms as the licensees did in fact move rooms. In *Antoniades v. Villiers* separate but identical agreements were

made with a couple asserting that no exclusive possession was granted and that the licensor or nominee could use the premises from time to time. The House of Lords found the latter provision was a pretence designed to evade the Rent Act. It had been intended for there to be exclusive possession so a valid lease did exist. In *Westminster City Council v. Clarke* [1992] 2 A.C. 288 the House of Lords held that the council had not granted exclusive possession to the occupant of a room in a hostel for the homeless. The council had denied exclusive possession by genuine terms such as the right to change the accommodation without notice. Exclusive occupation was also inconsistent with the purpose for which the Council had provided housing in the hostel.

Creation of Leases

KEY PRINCIPLE: *An agreement for a lease can be given effect in equity.*

Walsh v. Lonsdale 1882

The plaintiff and defendant agreed to a lease of a mill for seven years. The terms were to be those as stipulated in another lease. They included a term that rent was payable in advance on demand for a full year and any amount outstanding at the time of the demand. The plaintiff went into possession but paid rent quarterly in arrears. The defendant demanded a full year's advance rent plus the amount outstanding since the last payment and put in a distress. The plaintiff claimed that the distress was unlawful.

HELD: (C.A.) Since the Judicature Acts the court could in equity give effect to the agreement for a lease upon its intended terms. The court was not bound to recognize it only as a lease from year to year by payment of rent. If under the intended terms yearly rent was payable in advance on demand and demand was made then the distress was lawful. (1882) 21 Ch. 9.

COMMENTARY
If the lease had only been recognized at law as a yearly periodic one (and not a seven year lease because of the failure to seal it) the rent would have been payable in arrears. *Parker v. Taswell* (1858) 44 E.R. 1106 had already decided that equity could give effect to the intended terms of a

lease. The importance of *Walsh v. Lonsdale* is that it applies the Judicature Acts' principle that where there is a conflict between law and equity then equity should prevail. However, giving effect with an equitable remedy is still discretionary and subject to general equitable principles. In *Coatsworth v. Johnson* (1886) 55 L.J. Q.B. 220 the court refused specific performance of the agreed lease because the tenant was in breach of one of its covenants.

Covenants in Leases

KEY PRINCIPLE: *There is implied into every lease a covenant of quiet enjoyment.*

McCall v. Abelesz 1976
The plaintiff had a lease of part of a house. The defendants were the new landlords. They allowed for the gas, and also the water and a electricity for a time, to be left unconnected for a year and a half. The plaintiff had refused the landlord's offer of alternative accommodation. The plaintiff brought an action for harassment under the Rent Act.

HELD: (C.A.) The *Rent Act 1965* provisions as to harassment were penal but did not create a new cause of action. They also did not destroy existing civil remedies. [1976] Q.B. 585.

COMMENTARY
A claim for harassment can fall within the ambit of an action for breach of the landlord's implied covenant of quiet enjoyment. A physical interference or interruption of enjoyment can constitute breach.

KEY PRINCIPLE: *There is an implied term in leases that the lessor shall not derogate from grant.*

Harmer v. Jumbil (Nigeria) Tin Areas Ltd 1921
The plaintiff was granted a lease of land for the express purpose of storing explosives. The statutory licence provided that if buildings were erected within a certain distance the licence would be revoked. The defendants acquired a lease of neighbouring land from the same freeholder for the purpose of working minerals and to erect buildings for that purpose but

not in such a way as to interfere with the explosives store. The plaintiffs brought an action to restrain use of the mine and use of connected sheds.

HELD: (C.A.) The acts of the defendant could be imputed to the freeholder. Those acts were in derogation from the plaintiff's lease. It must be implied on the part of the freeholder not to do anything which would break the conditions under which the plaintiff held their explosives licence. [1921] 1 Ch. 200.

COMMENTARY
A breach of the covenant of quiet enjoyment will often also be a breach of the covenant against derogation though this will not be true in all cases.

KEY PRINCIPLE: *There is an implied term in leases that the property be fit for human habitation at the commencement of the lease.*

Smith v. Marrable 1843
A house was let. Upon taking possession the lessees found that it was infested with bugs.

HELD: (Exch) It is an implied condition in letting furnished property that it shall be reasonably fit for human habitation. Where it is not, the lessee may quit without notice. 152 E.R. 693.

COMMENTARY
This covenant gives the lessee the right to walk away from the lease at the time of its intended commencement without paying further rent and thereby gives the lessee a defence should the lessor seek to enforce the lease. Section 8(1) of the *Landlord and Tenant Act 1985* provides a statutory covenant that premises be and are kept fit for habitation. This, however, only applies to extremely low rent property and does not apply unless the renovation can be done at reasonable expense.

KEY PRINCIPLE: *There are statutorily implied covenants of repair by the lessor in some leases though these are interpreted restrictively.*

Quick v. Taff Ely Borough Council 1986

The plaintiff was tenant of a council flat. Severe condensation caused decoration, woodwork, furniture and bedding to rot. The condensation was caused by poor insulation and heating. The plaintiff brought an action for breach of the landlord's covenant to keep in repair the structure and exterior of the house implied by section 32(1) of the *Housing Act 1961*.

HELD: (C.A.) Liability under the implied covenant did not arise where there is a lack of amenity or inefficiency. It arises where there is a physical condition which requires repair. There was no damage or disrepair to the structure or exterior. The Council were not, therefore, liable for damage caused by condensation. [1986] Q.B. 609.

COMMENTARY

The equivalent statutorily implied covenant of repair in short leases, section 11(1) of the Landlord and Tenant Act 1985 as amended by section 116 (1) of the *Housing Act 1988*, has been also been restrictively interpreted. The standard of repair required is not objective but takes into account location, standard and life of the property. See *London Borough of Newham v. Patel* (1978) 13 H.L.R. 77.

KEY PRINCIPLE: *There is an implied contractual duty of care to keep common parts in reasonable repair and usability.*

Liverpool City Council v. Irwin 1977

Lessees of a ninth and tenth floor maisonette withheld their rent in protest at the condition of the block of flats. The lifts did not work, the staircases were unlit and the conditions appalling as a result of vandalism. The lessees' agreement did not specify terms as to repairing obligations of the common parts. The Council sought re-possession for non-payment of rent. The lessees counterclaimed that, *inter alia*, the Council owed a duty of care to keep the common parts in repair and properly lit.

HELD: (H.L.) In the absence of specific terms in the lease there was an obligation upon landlords to take reasonable care to keep means of access in reasonable repair and usability. This is subject the responsibilities of what reasonable lessees would do for themselves. The Council had made considerable effort and expense to deal with the problems caused by repeated vandalism. They were held not to be in breach of their obligation. The obligation applies to private and public landlords. [1977] A.C. 239.

COMMENTARY

The obligation is not absolute. The standard of the obligation is what is necessary in the circumstances. The obligation can be read narrowly to impose a minimal requirement that access to rented premises be kept as safe as is in the power of the landlord to make it. It could be read more widely to impose a catch-all duty on landlords to give effect to an agreement. If courts set a very high standard they could thereby impose a heavy burden on Councils and thus taxpayers. The case indicates that there are expectations of lessees and that there is a limit to the expense that Council's can be expected to make in dealing with vandalism.

In *Cavalier v. Pope* [1906] A.C. 428 it was held that a landlord was not liable for injury caused by defects at the commencement of a lease of unfurnished premises. The lessee's wife who was injured could not claim as she was not party to the contract. Nowadays, a landlord could be liable for injury caused by defects under legislation such as the *Occupiers Liability Act 1957* or *Defective Premises Act 1972* as well as in negligence.

KEY PRINCIPLE: *There are statutorily implied terms relating to unlawful eviction which provide a civil remedy as well as criminal sanctions.*

Tagro v. Cafane 1991

The plaintiff leased a bedsit from the defendant. There were incidents of harassment culminating in the plaintiff being excluded by the defendant, who changed the locks. The plaintiff obtained an injunction requiring the defendant to provide a new set of keys. These were made available only after an application was made to commit the defendant for failure to observe the injunction. Upon her return to the bedsit the plaintiff found her belongings damaged, destroyed or removed and the bedsit was wrecked. The plaintiff did not resume occupation and brought an action for unlawful eviction under sections 27 and 28 of the *Housing Act 1988*.

HELD: (C.A.) The act of providing keys together with the failure to restore the flat to its previous condition did not constitute reinstatement. The judge was entitled to take the plaintiff's valuation of the premises if the defendant did not adduce evidence to challenge it. [1991] 1 W.L.R. 378.

COMMENTARY

Though not decided, it is arguable that a plaintiff may choose whether to accept reinstatement. The test of damages in section 28 of the *Housing Act 1988* is the difference in value between the premises with a sitting tenant or the premises with vacant possession. The plaintiff's valuation of this at £31,000 was high but accepted by the court. In addition £15,000 was awarded in respect of damage to the plaintiff's belongings. The measure of damages is clearly designed to negative any financial gain to be made from unlawfully evicting a tenant. It is somewhat odd though in the sense that the penalty is awarded to the plaintiff.

KEY PRINCIPLE: *A number of "usual covenants" are implied into leases where not expressly provided for.*

Chester v. Buckingham Travel Ltd 1981

An agreement for a lease of garages was made by the parties. The plaintiff entered into occupation pending completion of the lease. The lease was made for 14 years though this was impossible to grant at the time of the agreement as the landlord was holding over under a previous head lease awaiting grant of a new one. The plaintiff brought proceedings for specific performance of the lease. The parties could not agree the terms of the lease and the matter was referred to the judge to determine what covenants should be included as the usual covenants in a lease.

HELD: (Ch.D.)

[i] The established usual covenants in a lease are for the lessee to pay rent, pay taxes except where expressly payable by the landlord, to keep and deliver up in good repair, and to allow the lessor to enter and view the state of repair. For the lessor, the usual covenant is the covenant of quiet enjoyment.

[ii] It is a question of fact to be determined by the court as to what additional usual covenants should be found in a

lease. In the context of a commercial lease of garage workshops, the only additional covenants should be that the tenant

[a] not alter the plan, height, elevation or appearance of the building without the landlord's consent;

[b] not obstruct windows or lights or knowingly permit any encroachment easements to be acquired;

[c] not alter the user of the premises without the landlord's consent, such consent not to be unreasonably withheld;

[d] not suffer any part of the premises to be a nuisance or cause annoyance to the neighbours.

The landlord has a right of re-entry for breach of covenant. [1981] 1 W.L.R. 96.

COMMENTARY
The nature of these additional covenants reflects the residential character of the area within which these workshops were situated.

Remedies for Breach of Landlord's Covenants in Leases

KEY PRINCIPLE: *Damages are intended to put the tenant in the position contracted for not to punish the landlord.*

Calabar Properties Ltd v. Stitcher 1984

The defendant took an assignment of a lease of a flat from the plaintiff. Due to defects on the outside, water was coming through causing damp and damage. The plaintiff asserted that the damp was caused by condensation. The plaintiff brought an action for non-payment of rent, the defendant counterclaimed that the plaintiff was in breach of his repair obligations. In the meantime the defendant and her husband moved out due to the husband's ill health caused by the damp. The judge held that the plaintiff was in breach of repair obligations and that the damage resulted from that breach. He awarded damages for the cost of making good and redecorating the flat less one third for betterment as well as for loss of enjoyment and the husband's ill-health. The judge refused to award damages to the defendant for rent, taxes or service charge during the period in which the premises were uninhabitable. He also refused damages for consequential loss of use during that period based on the capital value of the flat or its rental value.

HELD: (C.A.) The principle in assessing damages for breach of covenant is to restore the party to the position she would have been in had there been no breach of covenant. The judge properly assessed damages as the difference between the value of the flat to the defendant in the condition it was and the value it would have had to the defendant if the plaintiff had carried out his repair obligations. The cost of alternate accommodation during the period when the flat was uninhabitable was prima facie recoverable. Damages for outgoings were not recoverable as the lease was not terminated and the monies were still payable. Damages based on diminution of capital or rental value was inappropriate as the premises were rented as a home not a saleable asset. [1984] 1 W.L.R. 287.

COMMENTARY
A calculation as to rental of property in repair or disrepair may be relevant in calculating loss of enjoyment. A low rental cannot, however, be used to justify disrepair. In *Sturolson v. Mauroux* (1988) 20 H.L.R. 332 the plaintiff argued that damages awarded for disrepair should take into account the fair rent assessment on the premises. The court held that the measure of damages should reflect the property in a condition where the landlord carried out his repair obligations.

KEY PRINCIPLE: *Specific performance is available but the discretion to grant it should be exercised carefully.*

Jeune v. Queens Cross Properties Ltd 1974
In the lease between the parties there was an obligation upon the landlord to maintain, repair and renew the structure of the property, including the external walls. A balcony at the front of the building partially collapsed. The tenants claimed that the landlord was in breach of his obligation by failing to reinstate the balcony. The plaintiffs sought an order requiring immediate reinstatement of the balcony.

HELD: (Ch.D.) The court had the power to make an order for a landlord to carry out a specific piece of work under a repairing obligation. The discretion to grant such an order should be exercised carefully. [1974] 1 Ch. 97.

COMMENTARY
The breach must be clear and there must be no doubt as what is required to be done. An injunction could be given at inter-locutory hearings where there is a clear health hazard as in *Parker v. Camden LBC* [1986] Ch. 162.

KEY PRINCIPLE: *The remedy of self-help is available but does not allow the tenant to breach his own covenants.*

Lee-Parker v. Izzet 1971

The first defendant mortgaged properties to the plaintiff. The third and fourth defendant occupied some of these properties as tenants. They had contracts to buy the properties subject to mortgage arrangements being made. The plaintiff's mortgage had been made subject to these estate contracts. It became apparent that mortgage finance would not become available and that the first defendant now a bankrupt could not meet his mortgage loan repayments. The plaintiff seeking to protect his position agreed to honour the estate contracts providing that completion was made within one month. Failure to meet this stipulation would lead to repudiation of the contract and action for repossession. No sale took place and the plaintiff sought to repossess. The third and fourth defendants claimed that the first defendant had promised to effect certain repairs which had not been carried out.

HELD: (Ch.D.) The plaintiff's charge took subject to the third and fourth defendants' estate contract and rights thereunder. The contract was now repudiated and that repudiation was accepted. The third and fourth defendants could, however, recoup out of future rents the cost of repairs made by them-selves. [1971] 3 All E.R. 1099.

COMMENTARY
The repairs must have come within the landlord's express or implied obligations. Expenditure had to be proper on the facts. There is no right to withhold rent where the landlord is in default of repairing obligations. The remedy of self-help takes effect as a defence to an action for arrears of rent provided that it is clear that the obligation of the landlord was not being fulfilled and that reasonable expense has been incurred by the lessee in doing the repairs.

KEY PRINCIPLE: *In extreme cases a remedy of appointment of a receiver may be available.*

Hart v. Elmkirk 1983

The freeholder owned two blocks of flats which were let to lessees on long leases. The defendants bought the blocks. The blocks had fallen into disrepair, rent was not collected nor any contribution towards maintenance was sought. The lessees brought actions against the defendants to comply with their covenants and for damages. They also applied for an order that pending trial a surveyor should be appointed to accept rent and to manage the blocks in accordance with the land-lord's obligations.

HELD: (Ch.D.) Given the state of the buildings it would be just and convenient to appoint a receiver under section 37(1) of the *Supreme Court Act 1981*. [1983] 1 W.L.R. 1289.

COMMENTARY
This unusual remedy is useful where the landlord is not mak-ing repairs which leave the property at risk of progressive degradation.

Remedies for Breaches of Covenants in Leases by Tenants

[i] Forfeiture of lease

KEY PRINCIPLE: *The breach must be irremediable in the sense that it cannot be effectively remedied.*

Expert Clothing Service & Sales Ltd v. Hillgate House Ltd 1985

The plaintiffs granted the first defendant a lease for 25 years of premises which the defendant undertook to convert to a gym and health club. The second defendant was surety for the first defendant's liabilities. The rent fell into arrears and the plaintiff sought possession. The defendants brought proceedings to recover possession. These were settled and a consent order was made whereby the terms of the lease were varied. Under the new terms the defendants were required to notify the plain-tiff of their election to convert the premises to a gym or offices. They covenanted to substantially complete the re-construction by September 1982 and complete the work as soon as reason-ably possible thereafter. The first defendant charged the premises to a bank in breach of a covenant to give notice of any charges to the plaintiff. The plaintiffs refused to accept the rent due on the 29 September. They served notice on the defendant under section 146 of the *Law of Property Act 1925* claiming breach of covenant to re-construct by September 28, and breach of covenant not to charge the premises without giving notice. The plaintiffs asserted that the breaches were irremediable and required the defendants to quit and deliver up the premises. In October the plaintiffs' solicitors who acted for the plaintiffs in relation to the variation of the lease but not the section 146 notice sent a letter requesting that the defendants seal and execute the counterpart of the varied lease. The defendants now sought a declaration that this request constituted waiver of breach of covenant.

HELD: (C.A.) Breach of a positive covenant whether ongoing or singular was ordinarily capable of remedy by performance of the covenant and payment of compensation. The plaintiffs suffered no irremediable loss by the work being completed within a reasonable time thereafter. The section 146 notice was defective in not requiring the breach to be remedied. The plaintiffs were not entitled to possession. In the context of forfeiture proceedings being brought it was not reasonable to assume that the solicitor's letter in October indicated an intention on the plaintiff's behalf to treat the lease as subsisting. The plaintiffs had thus not waived their right to proceed with forfeiture. [1985] 2 All E.R. 998.

Traditionally, case law made a distinction that positive covenants were remediable but negative ones were not. Whilst this may in practice be often true the courts tend now not to ask whether the covenant is negative or positive but whether it can be put right. [1985] 2 All E.R. 998.

COMMENTARY

The case usefully serves to show that the purpose of the section 146 notice is to achieve a remedy for a breach insofar as it is possible, rather than to achieve forfeiture. This is reinforced by the requirement for a right of re-entry to be reserved in express leases, the availability of relief against forfeiture where a remedy is in fact given and/or where forfeiture is disproportionate, and the possibilities for stays on hearings and execution. See the Termination of Tenancies

Bill which if it comes into law will replace the present procedure and introduce the option of remedial orders or termination orders.

KEY PRINCIPLE: *Negative covenants are generally regarded as being irremediable.*

Scala House and District Property Co. Ltd v. Forbes 1974

In a lease of restaurant premises the lessees covenanted not to assign, sub-let or part with possession of the premises without the landlord's consent. The lease was assigned to the first defendant with consent. He intended to enter into an agreement with the second and third defendants to manage the restaurant but in fact created a sub-tenancy. The plaintiff who had bought the reversion served a section 146 notice requiring the breach to be remedied. After only 14 days he issued a writ for possession. At first instance it was held that the breach was remediable and that 14 days was insufficient to remedy the breach so the action would be dismissed.

HELD: (C.A.) Breach of a covenant not to assign, sub-let or part with possession without consent was not remediable. [1974] 1 Q.B. 575.

COMMENTARY
(1) Breach of the covenant not to assign without consent is regarded as the most clearly irremediable of covenants. This is because it involves a transfer of the property into the hands of someone unapproved. This is particularly troublesome as the lessee may have departed leaving outstanding liabilities whilst the occupying assignee may be unwittingly in default or not caring whether he is or not. In particular money remedies are not available against equitable assignees, *i.e.* where the assignment has not satisfied the required formalities. See however, *Bass Holdings Ltd v. Morton Music Ltd* [1987] 2 All E.R. 1001.
(2) In practical terms, the danger that the property will be allowed to fall into disrepair or worse leaves the landlord little effective remedy other than to forfeit the lease. Once a lease is forfeit all rights under the lease collapse. For a court to refuse forfeiture would be to impose on the landlord an unwanted occupant. In the present case, relief against forfei-

ture was in fact granted. Given that the plaintiff initially regarded the breach as being remediable, this seems appropriate.

KEY PRINCIPLE: *Breaches which put a stigma on the premises are irremediable.*

Rugby School (Governors) v. Tannahill 1935

The defendant lessee used the premises for the purpose of prostitution in breach of her covenant not to use the premises for illegal or immoral purposes.

HELD: (C.A.) Ceasing to so use the premises was not a remedy. The breach was irremediable in that the stigma was present. Failure to ask for a remedy did not invalidate the notice. Failure to ask for compensation did not invalidate the notice as the landlord is entitled not to ask for compensation. [1935] 1 K.B. 87.

COMMENTARY

Whilst not a common situation it is of practical importance that the law allows for tenants causing damage to the property in the sense of illegal or immoral use to be fairly swiftly removed.

KEY PRINCIPLE: *The court has discretion to grant relief against forfeiture.*

Shiloh Spinners v. Harding 1973

See also chapter 2 on Protection of Interests in Land. The plaintiffs assigned their lease in a mill to T Ltd, who made covenants as to fencing and support on their behalf and that of their successors. The plaintiffs had a right of re-entry in respect of breaches of covenant. T Ltd sold their interest in the premises to the defendants. T Ltd were absolved of any further liability in respect of the premises under the terms of the earlier assignment to them. The plaintiffs relying on their right of re-entry sought to regain possession against the defendant.

HELD: (H.L.) There was no general power to grant relief against a man's bargains. A court could, however, grant relief against forfeiture in limited circumstances where the primary objective of the bargain could be attained when the case came to court and where the forfeiture provision was a means of securing the objective of the bargain. Wilful breaches would only be rarely relieved against. Here, the breaches were substantial and showed a disregard for the plaintiff's rights. Relief was not therefore appropriate. [1973] A.C. 691.

COMMENTARY
Relief can be given if the purpose of the lease can be reinstated by putting right the breach provided the landlord/tenant relationship has not been fundamentally undermined. There has been a degree of merging of the tests of remediability and relief. A breach is remediable if it can effectively be remedied. Relief will be given where forfeiture is disproportionate and some remedy is made which restores the bargain.

KEY PRINCIPLE: *The court has jurisdiction to grant relief even after peaceable re-entry by the lessor where such re-entry was in the absence of the enforcement of a judgment for possession of the property.*

Billson v. Residential Apartments Ltd 1992
The tenants of an unoccupied property renovated in contravention of the landlord's express reservation of a right to prior written consent before such renovations could take place. The landlord's agents peaceably re-entered the property at 6 a.m. and changed the locks. They also affixed notices stating that the lease had been forfeited. The tenants' workmen regained possession of the property by breaking in four hours later. The question arose as to whether the court had jurisdiction to grant relief.

HELD: (H.L.) That the court had the jurisdiction to grant relief even after peaceable re-entry where such re-entry occured without the enforcement of a judgment for the possession of the property. [1992] 1 A.C. 494.

COMMENTARY
The case makes it clear that the court's jurisdiction to grant relief ends where the lessor re-enters the premises in execution of a "final, unappealed and fully executed" judgment for the possession of the property. Up until that time, the court retains the discretion to grant relief against forfeiture of the lease. It should be noted that both the Court of Appeal and the House of Lords in this case were unhappy with the method in

which recovery of the possession of the property was sought.

KEY PRINCIPLE: *Waiver of breach defeats an action for forfeiture.*

Segal Securities Ltd v. Thoseby 1963

By a lease the lessee covenanted to use the premises as a "private residence in the occupation of one household only." The lessee took in non paying "guests." She also took in a paying "guest" who had taken up residence in response to a newspaper advert. The landlord served a section 146 notice requiring remedy within 28 days. Between service of that notice and its expiry the landlord sent a demand for rent in a letter headed "without prejudice."

The letter went on to say that the demand was without prejudice to the service of notice or any breach of covenant. The lessee sent a cheque in payment but it was returned. The landlord issued a writ for possession.

HELD: (Q.B.D.) The lessee was in breach of covenant. The landlord had, however, waived that breach. A demand for rent is as good as acceptance of rent. An acceptance cannot be without prejudice so neither can a demand. Where rent is payable in advance demand or acceptance constitutes waiver only in respect of past and ongoing breaches known at the time. [1963] 1 Q.B. 887.

COMMENTARY

The applicable principle is that a landlord cannot forfeit if he has done an act indicating that the landlord tenant relationship is still in existence. To receive rent indicates an intent to remain a landlord. Waiver does not indicate approval of the breach and other remedies may still be available. An interesting case is *Van Haarlem v. Kasner* [1992] 64 P.&C.R. 214. where the landlord was held to have waived the lessee's breach of covenant not to use the premises for illegal activities. The tenant was arrested and subsequently convicted of espionage offences. The landlord's acceptance of rent after the arrest was held to have affirmed the lease. The case illustrates the importance of waiver in that it prevents a subsequent action for forfeiture even when the lessee was convicted. The presumption of innocence seems not to apply in the context of breach of covenant!

[ii] Other remedies

Instead of applying for forfeiture of the lease, the lessor can opt for the normal common law or equitable remedies against the lessee for breaches of covenants in the lease.

Transfer of Obligations in Leases

KEY PRINCIPLE: *At common law, subject to contrary agreement, a tenant remained liable to the landlord after he assigned his interest.*

Centrovincial Estates plc v. Bulk Storage Ltd 1983

A lease was granted for 21 years at a rent of £17,000 per annum. The rent was to be reviewed after 14 years in December 1978. In July 1978 the defendant assigned the remainder of his term. The plaintiff who was assignee of the reversion agreed with the assignee of the lease for the rent to be raised to £44.000. There was a default of rent and the plaintiff sought to recover from the defendant.

HELD: (Ch.D.) The rent agreement was properly made within the rent review clause of the lease. The assignee was not an agent of the lessee. The relationship between a landlord and an assignee was sui generis. An assignee owned the leasehold estate and could part with, alter its terms or deal with it as he wished to the extent consistent with being estate owner. The assignee could use the estate just as the original lessee could have done. By privity of contract a lessee remains liable after assignment. The lessee is liable for the lease even as altered because the lease allowed for alteration. The original lessee was liable for the rent as revised. (1983) 46 P. & C.R. 393.

COMMENTARY

This principle is altered by section 5 of the *Landlord and Tenant (Covenants) Act 1995* whereby the landlord cannot sue the original lessee in relation to breaches by the assignee. The landlord may require a guarantee from the original lessee in relation to the first assignee by section 16. By section 18 the original lessee cannot be liable for variations in the lease. Before this legislation courts were often reluctant to enforce the tenant's ongoing liability. See *City of London Corporation v. Fell* [1993] 2 W.L.R. 710 and *R.P.H. Ltd v. Mirror Group Newspapers and Mirror Group Holdings* (1992) 65 P. & C.R. 252 .

The converse of the common law position as to lessees is that a landlord remains liable to a tenant after he assigns his interest unless there is contrary expression. For example landlords' covenants are often expressed to bind the owner of the reversion for the time being. Under the new Act landlords can apply for release from covenants.

KEY PRINCIPLE: *At common law the benefit and burden of covenants passes to an assignee in respect of covenants which touch and concern the land.*

Spencer's Case 1583

A lessee covenanted for himself, his executors and administrators that he, his executors or assignees would build a wall on part of the land.

HELD: (K.B.) The covenant would not bind the lessee's assignees. (1583) 5 Co. Rep. 16a.

COMMENTARY

The covenant must relate to the land. Even if assignees are named the covenant must touch and concern the land. The covenant must not be personal or collateral to the agreement. What touches and concerns is usually easily recognised, *e.g.* an obligation to pay rent. It can, however, be problematic as to whether an option touches and concerns. See *Beesly v. Hallwood Estates* [1960] 1 W.L.R. 549. In relation to landlords the principle is confirmed in statute by sections 141, 142 of the *Law of Property Act 1925* whereby the benefit and burden of covenants runs to an assignee of the reversion.

The *Landlord and Tenant (Covenants) Act 1995* provides by section 2 that all terms of new leases pass upon assignment.

KEY PRINCIPLE: *At common law the benefit and burden of covenants runs to an assignee of the lease where there is privity of estate.*

Purchase v. Lichfield Brewery 1915

A lessee purported to assign the remainder of his lease. No deed was executed.

HELD: (K.B.D.) There was no privity of estate nor privity of contract between the landlord and the assignees. The assignees were not liable, therefore, to pay rent. [1915] 1 K.B. 184.

COMMENTARY

Privity of contract could in common law justify the ongoing liability of tenants. It also meant that assignees not being contractors would not be liable. The concept of privity of estate was developed to hold assignees of the lease liable. Privity of estate depends on the assignee being privy to the same estate as was the original lessee. Here although the original lease was legal, the assignment was not. Assignments are required by section 52 of the *Law of Property Act 1925* to be made by deed. Sub-lessees are different from assignees in that they take less than the full remainder of the term or less than the entire premises, they are similar in that they do not have privity of estate. Equitable assignees and sub-lessees cannot be liable for money remedies in relation to breach of covenant. The landlord may seek forfeiture of the original lease. If forfeited, all rights claimed under that lease collapse. Injunctions may be granted to restrain further breach of negative covenants. See *Tulk v. Moxhay* (1848) 41 E.R. 1143 (above).

The rules as to transfer of lessees' liabilities and the availability of remedies have often left landlords in a very difficult position. For example, if the tenant assigns without permission and the assignment is not in writing, the assignee breaches terms which he may not know exist or much less care. If the landlord has no right of re-entry or has somehow waived then forfeiture is unavailable. The equitable assignee is immune from money remedies. The original lessee may have disappeared. It is not surprising that the courts have occasionally tried to enforce covenants more fully against assignees of leases. See *Boyer v. Warbey* [1953] 1 Q.B. 234 where it was put that the distinction between assignments by deed or hand should not determine the transfer of obligations. The *Landlord and Tenant (Covenants) Act 1995* makes considerable changes to the law. The old law is still important as the

Act only applies to new leases except in claims for arrears of rent where the Act applies to both existing and new leases.

7. LICENCES

Introduction

Licences fall into four categories:
  Bare Licences
  Contractual Licences
  Licences coupled with an interest
  Licences coupled with an equity.

Bare Licence

KEY PRINCIPLE: *A bare licence is a mere permission to use another's land without further duty on either side.*

Holden v. White 1982
A milkman using a right of way to deliver milk was injured when he stepped on a broken manhole.

HELD: (C.A.) The landowner owed no duty of care to a person exercising such a right. [1982] Q.B. 679.

COMMENTARY
A bare licence is implied to walk up to a landowner's front door. This can extend to persons making deliveries or election canvassers as in *Evans v. Forsyth* (1979) 90 D.L.R. 3d 155. The licence is given without consideration and involves no further liabilities.

KEY PRINCIPLE: *A bare licence not being an interest in land is revocable at the will of the licensor.*

Wood v. Leadbitter 1845
The plaintiff bought a ticket for the enclosure at the Doncaster races. The defendant ordered him to leave. The plaintiff refused and was forcibly removed.

HELD: (Exch) Notwithstanding that a ticket had been bought it was still lawful for the licensor to revoke the licence without returning the fee and without giving reasons. Having been ordered to leave, the plaintiff was no longer at the place by leave or licence of the defendant. The eviction without unnecessary force was therefore not an assault. [1843-60] All E.R. Rep. 190.

COMMENTARY
The traditional view has been that a licence is revocable at will. The earlier cases did not appear to distinguish between bare and contractual licences. This case was decided prior to the *Judicature Acts 1873 and 1875* and would probably now be regarded as a case concerning a contractual licence (see later).

KEY PRINCIPLE: *When a bare licence is revoked, sufficient time must be allowed for the licensee to leave.*

Robson v. Hallett 1967

Three police officers came up to the defendant's front door. One was allowed to enter. The defendant's father then asked him to leave. He began to leave but was attacked by the first defendant before he exited. The other two officers came to his rescue. The first defendant assaulted both of them. The second defendant assaulted one of them. On appeal against conviction the defendants argued that the police officers were not acting in the course of their duty.

HELD: (C.A.) There is an implied licence to any member of the public coming on lawful business to come up to a front door and knock on it. The officers who entered the premises under this licence (which in respect of them had not been revoked) were acting in the course of their duty when coming to the help of their colleague. When a licence is revoked in a way requiring the licensee to act, then sufficient time must be allowed for that act. [1967] 2 Q.B. 939.

COMMENTARY
The implied licence to approach a front door can be expressly denied by a notice.

Licence Coupled with an Interest

KEY PRINCIPLE: *A licence coupled with a grant of a proprietary interest is not revocable whilst the interest subsists.*

Doe d. Hanley v. Wood 1819

The grantee was given by deed the right to dig for tin.

HELD: (K.B.D.) There was no lease of the land but a licence to dig for tin. The grantor re-entered the land lawfully within the terms of the licence. [1814-23] All E.R. 136.

COMMENTARY

The case is used as authority for the principle stated above, though it is far from clear if that is what the case decides. The right to use the land was in effect terminated, though *per curiam* it was said that the licence to search and extract tin is irrevocable in so far as the tin ore was actually extracted. The logic behind the principle is that a proprietary interest is not revocable so it would be inconsistent to allow the revocation of a licence which facilitates the use of the prorietary right.

Contractual Licence

KEY PRINCIPLE: *A contractual licence confers no interest in land and binds only the parties to it and not the land.*

Clore v. Theatrical Properties Ltd. 1936

The agreement granted rights to refreshment rooms in a theatre. It was described as a lease for the "free and exclusive use" of the rooms. However, this was limited to supply and accommodation of visitors to the the theatre "and for no other purpose whatsover." The agreement was assigned in defiance of a clause requiring consent for assignment. The owners of the theatre sought to stop the assignees from exercising rights under the agreement.

HELD: (C.A.) The agreement was a licence not a lease and could only be enforced as between the original parties to whom there was privity of contract.[1936] 3 All E.R. 483.

King v. David Allen & Sons Ltd 1916

The defendant granted the plaintiff a licence to affix advertising posters to a building as yet unbuilt. The defendant leased the land to a company. It appeared as if there had been a intention to assign the licence to the new landowner but no reference to it was incorporated into the lease. The company refused the permission granted in the licence.

HELD: (H.L.) The licence confered no interest in land. The licence bound the contracting parties and not the successor in title to the land. The licensor was liable for breach of contract having put it out of his power to honour the contract. [1916] 2 A.C. 54.

COMMENTARY

The traditional formulation of the law is found in *Thomas v. Sorrell* (1673) Vaugh. 330 where Vaughan C.J. stated that "a dispensation or licence properly passeth no interest, nor alters or transfers property in anything, but only makes an action lawful, which without it had been unlawful."

KEY PRINCIPLE: *Depending on its nature and terms, a contractual licence may be revocable.*

Winter Garden Theatre (London) Ltd v. Millennium Productions Ltd 1948

Winter Garden granted Countess Mala de la Marr a licence to use their theatre for a period of six months for stage plays, concerts or ballets. The licence contained an option to continue for a further period of six months subject to an increased rent. It further stated that upon the expiration of these two periods of six months, the Countess would have the option of continuing with the licence on making a weekly payment and that the Countess was to give Winter Garden one month's notice to terminate the licence. Winter Garden continued to manage the bars and cloak room. Millennium Productions Ltd ("Millennium") was incorporated by the Countess and with the consent of Winter Garden, the licence was assigned to it. On September 1945 Winter Garden served a notice terminating the licence on Millennium. Millennium claimed that the licence was not revocable by Winter Garden except where it had breached the terms of the licence or alternatively that it was valid for a reasonable period after the notice of revocation.

HELD: (H.L.) That the licence was not one which was perpetual in nature and as such on Winter Garden giving Millennium the notice to terminate the licence, Millennium would have a reasonable time to withdraw. On the facts of the case, Millennium failed to prove that the period given by Winter Garden was unreasonable and that accordingly the notice of termination given by Winter Garden was valid. [1948] A.C. 173.

COMMENTARY

With regards to the revocability of contractual licences the traditional view was that such licences were revocable (*Wood v. Leadbitter*). However, recent cases have suggested that such licences are not revocable until the contract has been performed. In *Hurst v. Picture Theatres Ltd* [1918] 1 K.B. 1, the Court of Appeal held that the plaintiff was entitled to damages, having been forcibly removed from a cinema before the film had ended. It has been said that the reason for this is that there is an implied term in the contract that the licence will not be revoked until the contract has been performed. This was the approach taken by Megarry J. in *Hounslow LBC v. Twickenham Garden Developments* [1971] Ch. 233. The decision of the House of Lords in *Winter Garden* makes it clear that whether such a term is implied into a contractual licence is ultimately a question of interpretation of the terms of the licence. Where a contractual licence is found to exist, the equitable remedies of specific performance or injunction may be available: *Verrall v. Great Yarmouth Borough Council* [1981] Q.B. 202.

KEY PRINCIPLE: *In some cases the court may be prepared to infer the existence of a contractual licence.*

Tanner v. Tanner 1975

A woman gave up a protected tenancy in order to move into her lover's home and to care for the children of the relationship.

HELD: (C.A.) A contractual licence was inferred in her favour which gave her the right to stay in the property for so long as the children were of school age and the accomodation was reasonably required. [1975] 1 W.L.R. 1346.

COMMENTARY

A similar approach was taken in *Chandler v. Kerley* [1978] 1 W.L.R. 693 where a contractual licence was inferred. On the facts of that case, the court held that the licence could be terminated only on giving reasonable notice.

Licence Coupled With an Equity

KEY PRINCIPLE: *A licence coupled with an equity may be enforceable against a third party.*

Errington v. Errington & Woods 1952

A father bought a house in his own name. He promised his son and daughter that if they paid the loan instalments they could live in the house and when the final payment was made he would transfer the title to them. The father died and left all his property including the house to his widow. The son left the house to live with his mother. The daughter in law continued to live in the house and pay the loan instalments. The mother brought an action for possession against the daughter in law.

Held: (C.A.) The son and daughter in law were licensees under a personal contract entitled to remain in the house so long as they paid the instalments. Lord Denning went further in characterising the right as an equitable one which would grow into an equitable interest once the mortgage loan was repaid.[1952] 1 K.B. 290.

COMMENTARY
(1) The ground for making the contractual licence of occupation irrevocable is that equitable jurisdiction should intervene to prevent a breach of contract. The principle in *Wood v. Leadbitter* can be dealt with by arguing that before the fusion of courts of equity and common law, injunctive relief would not have been available or on the facts an injunction would not be practically feasible. Here, Lord Denning found cause to invoke the jurisdiction in what is called a licence coupled with an equity. This can be seen as analogous to a licence coupled with an interest where the licence cannot be revoked whilst the interest subsists. The argument goes that a licence should not be revoked where it is coupled with an equity. The equity could be found in an implied term not to revoke or in a putative beneficial interest or in an estoppel-type argument that detriment and reliance should prevent revocation. Much of the problem with this case is that it is not clear if there is a single agreed equity which is being relied on.
(2) The case does not need to decide whether there is a need to transfer title once the instalments are paid. Lord Denning took the view that once paid there would be a beneficial interest in the house in favour of the son and daughter in

law. How the equity not to revoke transforms to an equitable interest in the property is not apparent, given the shaky basis for the equity against revocation itself. It could be argued on proprietary estoppel or constructive trust grounds though which or either is not clear.

(3) The most problematic aspect of this case is the impact it has on the third party. It is established law that a licence is contractual and thus binding on the parties only. Here the so called equity is used as the ground for making the licence irrevocable. That irrevocability turns the so-called equity into an interest binding on a third party, the widow. Being binding, that interest takes on the character of a proprietary interest.

KEY PRINCIPLE: *A spouse does not have a proprietary interest in the matrimonial home simply by virtue of being a spouse.*

National Provincial Bank v. Ainsworth 1965

The husband left his wife. The matrimonial home was charged to a bank who were owed £6,000. The husband incorporated his business and transfered the home and business premises to the company. The liability for the loan now lay with the company rather than the husband personally. The loan was defaulted on and the bank gained a re-possession order. The wife sought recission of the re-possession order .

HELD: (H.L.) The rights of the deserted wife were personal. They were not proprietary rights which could bind a transferree irrespective of whether the rights preceded those of the transferee or not. A wife's rights to occupy a matrimonial home arising from family law do not confer proprietary rights.[1965] A.C. 1175.

COMMENTARY
In the Court of Appeal in *National Provincial Bank v. Hastings Car Mart* [1964] Ch. 665 on the same facts it was held that a husband was presumed to have given authority to a wife to remain in the matrimonial home and that the deserted wife's right to remain was a licence coupled with an equity which would then bind a transferree.

KEY PRINCIPLE: *A contractual licence has been held to be an equitable interest which the court will protect.*

Binions v. Evans 1972

The defendants husband previously occupied a cottage in return for service. When the husband died the trustees agreed to permit the widow "to reside in and occupy" the cottage as "tenant at will . . . for the remainder of her life." The trustees sold the estate to the plaintiffs incorporating a clause in the conveyance to protect the widow's occupation. The plaintiff sought possession.

HELD: (C.A.) The terms of the agreement were inconsistent and did not create a tenancy at will but did according to Lord Denning create a contractual licence resulting in an equity binding on the plaintiff. The owner held the estate on constructive trust to permit the defendant to remain during her life for as long as she wished.[1972] Ch. 359.

COMMENTARY

This case represents the height of the enforcement of contractual licences. It, like many other cases, breaks the principle that a contractual licence is revocable and such breach is actionable in contract only. It goes against the principle of privity of contract that a contract should bind the parties only. By saying that the equity binds a third party it gives the contract a proprietary character which it should not have. Moreover, it defies principles of registration of proprietary interests. On the facts of this case a just result has been achieved at the expense of a tortuous and unnecessary interpretation of the authorities. It would have been easier to infer a tenancy which would bind the purchaser because of them being estopped by their knowledge of the special clause in the conveyance from claiming a failure to register. In *Midland Bank v. Farmpride Hatcheries Ltd* (1980) 260 E.G. 493 the court appeared to accept without question that a contractual licence was fully capable of binding a purchaser of the land provided he had notice of the licence. Fortunately, this must be *obiter* as the purchaser was found to have no notice.

KEY PRINCIPLE: *An agreement for a licence can be construed as a tenancy which then does bind the land. A licence can alternatively be binding under a constructive trust.*

Ashburn Anstalt v. W J Arnold & Co. 1989

The defendant sold his lease on a shop. The agreement provided that he could remain in the property as licensee for six months. The purchaser agreed to offer the defendant a new lease of a shop once the premises were redeveloped. Before the six months were up the plaintiff bought the freehold. Though the purchase was subject to the defendant's agreement the plaintiff sought to repossess. At first instance it was held that the defendant's agreement constitued a binding licence.

HELD: (C.A.) Though expressed to be a licence the agreement in fact constituted a tenancy. The plaintiff was therefore bound. The defendant had an overriding interest of actual occupation based on the proprietary interest in the tenancy. This did not entitle the defendant to prevent redevelopment of the property but did give him the right to an offer of a lease of a shop if the premises were so redeveloped. If the agreement was a licence it could not be binding as a licence, but could be enforced if there was evidence that the conscience of the owner should be affected with a constructive trust making it inequitable to revoke the licence. [1989] Ch. 1.

COMMENTARY

The case reaffirms the principle that a licence is not a proprietary right but offers a better ground for giving effect to the licence by constraining the owner rather than making the licence binding on the land. See Chap. 6, Leases for cases on the test for the distinction between leases and licences.

The case is important for the dicta of Fox L.J. with regard to the decision in *Errington v. Errington & Woods*. Fox L.J. stated that "[t]he far reaching statement of principle in *Errington* was not supported by authority, not necessary for the decision of the case and *per incuriam* in the sense that it was made without reference to authorities which, if they would not have compelled, would surely have persuaded the court to adopt a different ratio . . . the *Errington* rule . . . was neither practically necessary nor theorectically convincing."

8. MORTGAGES

Creation of Mortgages

KEY PRINCIPLE: *Equitable mortgages cannot be created by informal deposit of title deeds.*

United Bank of Kuwait v. Sahib

In 1992 the plaintiff obtained a charging order absolute over Sahib's interest in property which he jointly owned with his wife. This was to secure a judgment which the plaintiff had obtained against Sahib. However, it was subsequently discovered that in 1990, Sahib's solicitors had written to the third defendant confirming that they were holding the land certificate for that property to the third defendant's order as security for monies advanced to Sahib. The plaintiff sought a declaration that the third defendant did not hold any equitable mortgage over the property or that if it did, that such mortgage or charge did not take priority over the plaintiff's charging order. The judge found in the plaintiff's favour and the third defendant appealed.

HELD: (C.A.) Section 2 of the *Law of Property (Miscellaneous Provisions) Act 1989* required that a contract for the sale or disposition of an interest in land be in writing contained in a single document incorporating all the terms and signed by the parties. The effect of this section was to abolish the rule that a mortgage or charge could be created by the deposit to title deeds. The deposit of title deeds took effect as a contract to create a mortgage which fell within the ambit of section 2. Since there was no written document in this case, no mortgage or charge had been created and therefore the appeal would be dismissed.[1996] 3 All E.R. 215.

COMMENTARY

This case has clarified the application of section 2 of the *Law of Property (Miscellaneous Provisions) Act 1989* in that, with the possible exceptions of constructive/resulting/implied trusts and the doctrine of estoppel, all contracts for the sale and other disposition of an interest in land must be in writing.

The Equity of Redemption

KEY PRINCIPLE: *There must be no clogs or fetters on the equity of redemption—any attempt to exclude the equitable right to redeem will be void.*

Samuel v. Jarrah Timber and Wood Paving Corporation Ltd 1904

A company borrowed money upon the security of their debenture stock. This was subject to the lender having the option to purchase the stock within twelve months. The loan was repayable with interest upon giving thirty days' notice on either side. Before the company gave notice of its intention to repay the loan, the lender claimed the right to purchase the stock at the agreed price.

HELD: (H.L.) The option to purchase the stock was void and the company was entitled to redeem the loan on payment of all monies outstanding. [1904] A.C. 323.

COMMENTARY

In *Samuel v. Jarrah Timber and Wood Paving Corporation Ltd*, the court reluctantly decided that the option was void. The reason for the reluctance was because the option had been entered into by the two parties in an arms' length transaction, but, as the effect of the option was to deprive the mortgagor of his right to redeem the mortgage, the option had to be held to be void. The Earl of Halsbury L.C. suggested that if a day had intervened between the mortgage and the grant of the option, it would have been a perfectly good bargain. In the earlier case of *Reeve v. Lisle* [1902] A.C. 461, the House of Lords decided that where there was a gap of 10 days between the mortgage and the grant of the option to purchase the mortgaged property, the option was valid because the option could be regarded as a separate and independent transaction.

KEY PRINCIPLE: *Any provision in the mortgage which renders the equitable right to redeem illusory may be void.*

Fairclough v. Swan Breweries 1912

A mortgagor mortgaged a short lease of about 20 years as security for a loan. The loan repayments were by way of monthly instalments with the last instalment being payable about six weeks before the end of the lease. A provision in the mortgage prevented the mortgagor from repaying the monies outstanding other than by the agreed instalments. The mortgagor wished to redeem the mortgage early.

HELD: (P.C.) That for all practical purposes, this provision rendered the mortgage irredeemable and therefore, the mortgagor was entitled to early redemption of the mortgage.[1912] A.C. 565.

Knightsbridge Estates Trust Ltd v. Byrne 1938

The respondents mortgaged its property to the appellants as security for a loan at a favourable interest rate. The mortgage deed provided, *inter alia*, that the respondents were to repay the principal with interest by way of 80 half-yearly instalments and did not allow the mortgagor the right of early redemption. The respondents sought to pay off the loan early.

HELD: (C.A.) There was no rule against unreasonable postponement of the right to redeem. On the facts of the case, there were no provisions in the mortgage deed which could be considered to be onerous and unreasonable. There was therefore, no clog on the equity of redemption and the mortgagor was not entitled to redeem the mortgage early. [1938] 1 Ch. 441.

COMMENTARY

In *Knightsbridge Estates Trust Ltd v. Byrne*, the court was of the view that as this was an arms' length transaction between two competent parties with expert advice, and the mortgagor had negotiated the best terms available at the time, the mortgagor should be held to its bargain. Sir Wilfred Greene stated that "equity does not reform mortgage transactions merely because they are unreasonable." However, where the terms in the mortgage render the equitable right to redeem illusory, as in *Fairclough v. Swan Brewery Co.*, the court may be prepared to intervene.

Collateral Advantages

KEY PRINCIPLE: *Collateral advantage clauses in mortgages are void if they are unconscionable or a clog on the equitable right to redeem.*

Noakes v. Rice 1902

The respondent bought a lease of a public house from the appellants, who were brewers. This was with the help of a loan from the appellants, which was secured on a mortgage of the premises. The respondents covenanted, *inter alia*, that he and all persons deriving title under him would not during the term of the lease, and whether any money was or was not owning to the appellants under the mortgage loan, use or sell any malt liquors except such as should be purchased from the appellants.

HELD: (H.L.) The covenant was a clog on the equitable right to redeem and as such the respondents upon payment of all monies outstanding under the mortgage, was entitled to have the property reconveyed to him free of the collateral advantage. The collateral advantage was unenforceable after redemption of the mortgage.[1902] A.C. 24.

KEY PRINCIPLE: *A collateral advantage may be valid and enforceable, even after the redemption of the mortgage, if it is regarded as a contract which is collateral to the mortgage.*

G & C Kreglinger v. New Patagonia Meat and Cold Storage Company Ltd 1914

The appellants, a firm of wool brokers, agreed to lend money to the respondents, who were a company carrying on the business of meat preservers. The loan was secured by way of a floating charge on the respondents' assets. It was provided in the agreement that for a period of five years from the date of the loan, the respondents would not sell sheepskins to any person other than the appellants so long as they were willing to purchase the sheepskins at the best price offered by any other person. The loan was paid off by the respondents three years after the loan was taken out. The appellants purported to exercise their option to purchase the sheepskins.

HELD: (H.L.) The appellants' option to buy the sheepskins from the respondents was not part of the mortgage transaction but formed a collateral contract which was entered into as a condition for the grant of the loan. In the circumstances of the case, the option was not a clog on the equitable right to redeem and because it was a separate contract from the mortgage, the option was enforceable even after the mortgage had been redeemed. The appellants were entitled to an injunction restraining the respondents from selling the sheepskins to any person other than the appellants.[1914] A.C. 25.

COMMENTARY

G & C Kreglinger v. New Patagonia Meat and Cold Storage Company Ltd. is important because it makes it clear that if the collateral advantage is regarded as a separate contract, but one which is collateral to the mortgage, the collateral advantage is valid. More importantly, it can continue for the duration for which the advantage had been granted even after the mortgage is redeemed. Further, Lord Parker suggested that a collateral advantage would be valid provided that it was not [a] unfair or unconscionable; or [b] in the nature of a penalty clogging the equity of redemption; or [c] inconsistent with or repugnant to the contractual or equitable right to redeem. See also other cases such as *Biggs v. Hoddinott* [1898] 2 Ch. 307.

Unconscionable Bargains

KEY PRINCIPLE: *The court has jurisdiction to grant relief against harsh or unconscionable terms in mortgages.*

Cityland and Property (Holdings) Ltd v. Dabrah 1968

A tenant who lived in a property for 11 years was offered the property by the landlord for £3,500. As the tenant had only £600, it was agreed that £2,900 would be left owing on mortgage. The terms of the mortgage was that a total of £4,553 was to be repaid in 72 monthly instalments. In the event of a default the whole sum became due and payable. The landlord sought an order for the repayment of all monies outstanding, possession of the property and an order for sale.The tenant alleged that the terms of the advance were unreasonable and oppressive and that the large premium payable was harsh and unconscionable.

HELD: (Ch.D.) That the premium payable amounted to an effective annual interest rate of 19 per cent. Further, the provision that upon default the whole amount would be due and payable meant that the premium would amount to 57 per cent of the sum lent.The premium was so large that it was out of all proportion to the interest rates prevailing at the time the loan was made. In the circumstances this was unreasonable. The landlord would be entitled to enforce payment of the principal sum with interest at 7 per cent after taking into account the instalments already paid. [1968] 1 Ch. 166.

Multiservice Bookbinding v. Marden 1979

The defendant granted to the plaintiff a loan of £36,000 secured by a mortgage of the plaintiff's business premises. The terms of the mortgage provided, *inter alia*, that the capital was repayable by way of instalments over a 10-year period with interest at the rate of 2 per cent above the prevailing bank rate. It also provided by clause six that the sum payable as principal or interest was to be index linked to the Swiss franc. A declaration was sought as to whether clause six was void and unenforceable as being contrary to public policy and whether all the terms of the mortgage taken together were unenforceable.

HELD: (Ch.D.) The relevant test to decide whether a term in the contract was objectionable was whether the term was unfair and unconscionable. It was not sufficient to show that the term was unreasonable. On the facts of the case, clause six was not contrary to public policy. The parties were of equal bargaining power so that whilst the terms in the mortgage may be unreasonable, they were not unfair or unconscionable. The court would not intervene to relieve the plaintiffs of their obligations under the terms of the mortgage.[1979] 1 Ch. 84.

COMMENTARY

The plaintiff in *Multiservice Bookbinding Ltd v. Marden*, may have been unfortunate because of the variation in the exchange rate between the Swiss franc and the pound sterling between the date of the mortgage (12.07 5/8 francs to a £1) and the date of redemption of the mortgage (about 4 francs to a £1). However, Browne Wilkinson J. was clear that in order for the clause to be held to be void, it had to be harsh and unconscionable in the circumstances of the case.

KEY PRINCIPLE: *An extortionate credit agreement may be reopened by the court under sections 137–139 of the* Consumer Credit Act 1974.

Woodstead Finance Ltd v. Petrou 1986

Mrs Petrou obtained a loan of £25,000 for a period of six months in order to help her husband's finances. This was secured by a mortgage of her home. Woodstead Finance Ltd imposed an interest rate which was equivalent to annual rate of 42.5 per cent because of the husband's bad record in repayments.

HELD: (C.A.) The interest rate imposed was not extortionate in view of the husband's payment record and the risks which had been taken by the finance company.[1986] F.L.R. 158.

COMMENTARY

Although it would appear that the application of sections 137–139 of the *Consumer Credit Act 1974* appears to be restrictive, it is not necessarily so. This is because section 137 directs the court to have regard to the experience, age, business capacity and the degree under which the borrower was subjected to financial pressure and the degree of risk accepted by the lender in deciding whether the credit agreement is extortionate. The court applied the criteria laid down in the Act and considered that on the facts of the case, the credit agreement was not extortionate. Likewise in *A Ketley Ltd v. Scott* [1980] C.C.L.R. 37, the borrowers, a husband and wife, obtained a loan from the plaintiff at an interest rate of 12 per cent over three months (which equated to an annual rate of 48 per cent). They subsequently applied to set aside the agreement. It was decided that an annual interest rate of 48 per cent was not to be regarded as extortionate under the 1974 Act, since on the facts of the case, the husband, because of his business experience, had known what he was doing. They had not been subjected to any financial pressure to enter into the agreement.

Fraud and Undue Influence

KEY PRINCIPLE: *There must be no fraud, undue influence or misrepresentation which induced the mortgagor to mortgage the property to the mortgagee.*

National Westminster Bank v. Morgan 1985

A husband and wife signed a charge over their matrimonial home as security for a loan. The wife signed the charge in the presence of the bank manager who had visited the house for the purpose. The atmosphere during the visit was tense with the wife being concerned about the effect of the charge. She nonetheless signed the document. When the husband failed to repay the loan, the bank commenced possession proceedings. The wife alleged that the bank manager had exercised undue influence over her when her signature on the charge was obtained.

HELD: (H.L.) In order for a transaction to be set aside on the basis of undue influence, whether actual or presumed, it must be shown that the transaction had been wrongful in that it constituted a manifest and unfair disadvantage to the person seeking to set aside the transaction. On the facts of the case, there was no evidence that the relationship between the wife and the bank had ever gone beyond that of a bank and its customer and the transaction was not disadvantageous to the wife. Accordingly, the order for possession made at first instance would be reinstated.[1985] 1 A.C. 686.

KEY PRINCIPLE: *A transaction can be set aside on the basis of fraud, undue influence or misrepresentation where the person who has exercised the fraud, undue influence or misrepresentation over the mortgagor or co-mortgagor is an agent of the mortgagee.*

Barclays Bank v. Kennedy 1989

The appellant's husband was part of a group seeking to take-over the business the company which employed him. The husband agreed to guarantee the personal overdraft of the owner of the company and secure it by way of a charge on his matrimonial home. When the husband attended at the bank to execute the charge and guarantee, he was informed that the appellant's signature would also be required. The husband did not tell the appellant until 3 p.m. on the day which she was to sign the charge. She arrived at the bank just before close of business. The bank sought to enforce the charge. The appellant alleged that her signature had been procured by the husband acting as agent for the bank.

HELD: (C.A.) The bank would be liable for the undue influence of the husband where it had been content to leave it to the husband to secure the appellant's signature on the basis that as the charge was to her manifest disadvantage, the bank could not divest itself of vicarious liability for the husband's actions.

The appellant's appeal was allowed and a retrial was ordered on the question of whether there was undue influence and misrepresentation.(1989) 58 P.&C.R. 221.

COMMENTARY

It would in many cases be difficult, and in some cases artificial, to allege that the husband or partner was acting as an agent of the bank where undue influence or misrepresentation is alleged. In the light of *Barclays Bank v. O'Brien* (below), this is no longer necessary.

KEY PRINCIPLE: *The mortgagee can be liable for the fraud, undue influence or misrepresentation committed by one co-mortgagor on the other co-mortgagor where the mortgagee has constructive notice of the co-mortgagor's actions and the transaction is to the innocent co-mortgagor's manifest disadvantage.*

Barclays Bank v. O'Brien 1994

The husband persuaded his wife to mortgage her share of the family home as security for a business loan from the bank. The manager at the bank sent the documentation to another branch for the husband and wife to sign, with instructions to ensure that the parties were aware of the effect of the transaction and to seek independent legal advice if in doubt. The instructions were not complied with. The husband told his wife that the mortgage would be for a short duration and limited to £60,000. In fact, it was a long-term loan and the mortgage covered an unlimited liability. The bank sought an order for possession and sale of the property. The wife alleged that her signature on the charge had been procured by undue influence.

HELD: (H.L.) Where a spouse or cohabitee stood as a surety for the debts of the other, which was to the former's manifest disadvantage, and the creditor was aware of the relationship between them, the surety's obligation would be invalid where the surety was induced to act by the undue influence, misrepresentation or other legal wrong of the principal debtor. The creditor would in this situation be fixed with constructive notice of the principal debtor's wrongdoing unless it had taken reasonable steps to satisfy itself that the surety entered into the obligation freely. This obligation would be discharged if it had warned the surety of the extent of her liability and the risks involved and advised to seek independent legal advice. On the facts of the case, the bank should have been put on inquiry as to the circumstances of the case and in view of its failure to warn her of the risks and advise her to seek independent legal advice, the bank was fixed with constructive notice of the husband's misrepresentation. The wife was therefore entitled to set aside the charge. [1994] 1 A.C. 180.

COMMENTARY

(1) The House of Lords took the view that the relationship between the husband and wife fell within the category of cases where undue influence would be presumed because of the *de facto* relationship of trust and confidence between them.

(2) Their Lordships made it clear that the provision of written warnings by the bank to the surety was not enough to avoid being fixed with constructive notice. It was recognised that such notices were rarely effective. The steps to be taken by the Bank in order to avoid being fixed with notice of the husband's wrongdoing would include conducting a private interview with the wife in the husband's absence and warning her of the risks involved and advised her to seek independent legal advice. The requirement of a private interview in the husband's absence has not been followed in later cases where it has been held that the bank's obligation is discharged if it had warned the wife or cohabitee to seek independent legal advice or had received a confirmation from the solicitors that such legal advice had been given. See cases such as *Midland Bank v. Serter* [1994] E.G.C.S. 45, *Midland Bank v. Greene* [1993] N.P.C. 152, *Bank of Baroda v. Rayarel, The Times*, January 19, 1995, and *Barclays Bank v. Thomson, The Independent*, November 15, 1996.

KEY PRINCIPLE: *The steps which have to be taken by the mortgagee in order to avoid constructive notice may depend on the facts of the case.*

Credit Lyonnais Bank v. Burch

The defendant used her property as security for her employer's business overdraft. The defendant alleged that she had been unduly influenced by her employer to enter into the transaction which was manifestly to her disadvantage. The plaintiff had advised her to take independent legal advice but the defendant had refused to do so.

HELD: (C.A.) The plaintiff was fixed with constructive notice of the employer's undue influence on the defendant to enter into a transaction which was to her manifest disadvantage. The steps which the plaintiff had taken was not sufficient to avoid constructive notice. Accordingly, the transaction would be set aside. [1997] 1 All E.R. 144.

COMMENTARY

The interesting point that emerges from this case is that the steps which a bank need to take in order to avoid constructive notice depends on the facts of the case. Merely advising the mortgagor to take independent legal advice on the facts of the present case was inadequate. The transaction was one which the bank should have been put on enquiry and should have obtained an assurance from her solicitor that such advice had in fact been given. That does not however overcome the difficulty faced by the bank, where as in this case, the person concerned refuses or waives the right to take independent legal advice. The safest approach for the bank in such cases would be to insist that confirmation be obtained from solicitors that legal advice had been given with respect to the transaction. In *Bank Melli Iran v. Samadi-Rad* [1995] N.P.C. 76, an assurance that such independent legal advice had been given was necessary in order to avoid constructive notice. More recently, in *Banco Exterior Internacional S.A. v. Thomas* [1997] 1 All E.R. 46, where the chargor charged her property in order to guarantee the debts of a personal friend in return for a regular income, the Court of Appeal refused to set aside the transaction. The bank had discharged its obligation by ensuring that the chargor received independent legal advice about the nature and effect of the transaction.

KEY PRINCIPLE: *The doctrine of constructive notice only applies in this context where the mortgage or charge is to the manifest disadvantage of the co-mortgagor alleging undue influence.*

CIBC Mortgages plc v. Pitt 1993

Mr and Mrs Pitt charged their home as security for a loan of £150,000 ostensibly for the proposed purchase of a holiday home. Mr Pitt, who had coerced his wife's agreement to the loan, took the money and invested it in shares on the stock exchange. CIBC sought possession of the property upon default of the loan repayments. Mrs Pitt argued that the charge was invalid because of the husband's undue influence.

HELD: (H.L.) In order for Mrs Pitt to set aside the legal charge against CIBC, she had to establish that CIBC was affected by her husband's wrongdoing either on the basis that he was CIBC's agent or that CIBC had actual or constructive notice of the husband's actions. In the present case, there was no evidence to show that the loan was anything other than to the joint benefit of Mr and Mrs Pitt. As such the loan was not to Mrs Pitt's manifest disadvantage and there was nothing which put CIBC on enquiry.[1993] A.C. 200.

COMMENTARY
In *Barclays Bank v. O'Brien*, the combination of the relationship between the parties and the fact that the transaction was to the co-mortgagor's manifest disadvantage put the bank on enquiry. In *CIBC Mortgages v. Pitt*, the transaction on the face of it was for the joint benefit of the parties and as such there was nothing which put the mortgagee on enquiry.

KEY PRINCIPLE: *It is a question of fact whether the mortgage is to the innocent mortgagor's manifest disadvantage.*

Goode Durrant Administration v. Biddulph 1994
The bank lent money to a company, the defendant and her husband jointly. The defendant had a 2.5 per cent share holding in the company with the husband holding 90 per cent of the shares. Her husband dealt with the bank on the company's behalf.

HELD: (Ch.D.) As the defendant had reposed trust and confidence in her husband, this gave rise to a presumption of undue influence. On the facts of the case, as the transaction involved a risk of incurring substantial personal liability for a small share in the profit, based on her share holding, the loan would be regarded as being to the defendant's manifest disadvantage. As the bank failed to take steps to avoid the imputation of constructive notice, the transaction would be set aside against the defendant.[1994] 2 F.L.R. 551.

COMMENTARY

This can be contrasted with *Barclays Bank v. Sumner* [1996] E.G.C.S. 65, where the wife had an equal share in the company's business together with her husband. The court decided that the transaction was not to the wife's manifest disadvantage as she had a direct financial interest in the company to the same extent as that of her husband's. It is apparent that the question of manifest disadvantage is a question of fact dependent on the circumstances of the case.

KEY PRINCIPLE: *Where property is mortgaged for a dual purpose and a co-mortgagor has received a benefit from one of these purposes, the mortgage will not be set aside on the basis of undue influence unless the innocent co-mortgagor repays the benefit received from the transaction.*

Dunbar Bank plc v. Nadeem 1996

The husband took out a loan of £260,000 out of which £210,000 was used to purchase a leasehold property with his wife, which was charged to the bank. The balance of £50,000 was to secure his personal debts with the bank. The bank applied for a possession order on the property upon the husband's default of the loan repayments. The wife applied for the bank's charge to be set aside on the basis of undue influence.

HELD: (Ch.D.) That the bank had constructive notice of the possibility of undue influence as the transaction was one which was disadvantageous to the wife. The bank had failed to ensure that the wife had received independent legal advice. However, it was proper in this case to order that the wife would not be entitled to set aside the charge until she had repaid £105,000, which represented the benefit which she obtained from the bank plus interest. [1997] 2 All E.R. 253.

KEY PRINCIPLE: *Where the undue influence, fraud or misrepresentation is established, the whole mortgage is set aside even though there may have been an agreement to be liable for a lesser amount.*

TSB v. Camfield 1995

Mrs Camfield was induced by her husband's innocent misrepresentation to stand surety and charged their matrimonial home as security for a business loan. The husband had told her that the maximum liability for the loan was limited to £15,000 when in fact it was unlimited.

HELD: (C.A.) The bank was fixed with constructive notice of the misrepresentations and as such the charge would have to be set aside. The bank was not entitled to an order that the charge be partially enforceable against Mrs Camfield. The House of Lords' decision in *Barclays Bank v. O'Brien* was not authority for such a proposition.[1995] 1 All E.R. 951.

COMMENTARY

Where a mortgage is set aside because of undue influence, fraud or misrepresentation, it is all or nothing process. The whole mortgage is set aside even though there may have been an agreement to be liable for a lesser amount. This has been followed by the Court of Appeal in *Castle Phillips Finance v. Piddington* [1995] 70 P. & C.R. 592.

Rights and Remedies of the Mortgagee

[a] To take possession

KEY PRINCIPLE: *The mortgagee's estate in land gives it the right in law to take possession immediately upon the creation of the mortgage unless the right has been impliedly or expressly postponed until default.*

Four-Maids Ltd v. Dudley-Marshall 1957

The defendant charged its property to the plaintiff to secure repayment of £6,000. The charge provided that the principal sum would not be recalled before December 17, 1958 if the mortgagor paid the interest within seven days after the date when it became due. On the defendant's failure to pay the interest within seven days after it became due, the plaintiff served a written notice requiring repayment of the principal sum and interest immediately. The plaintiff applied for an order for possession of the property.

HELD: (Ch.D.) The mortgagee has a right to possession of the property in the absence of an express or implied agreement to the contrary. This right arises because the mortgagee has a legal term of years or its statutory equivalent. As such the plaintiff was entitled to an order for possession of the property. [1957] 1 Ch. 317.

COMMENTARY
(1) Harman J. at 320 stated that the ". . . mortgagee may go into possession before the ink is dry on the mortgage unless there is something in the contract, express or by implication, whereby he has contracted himself out of that right."
(2) Examples of where there can be express or implied postponement of the right to possession or not, can be found in cases such as *Esso Petroleum Co Ltd v. Alstonbridge Properties Ltd* [1975] 1 W.L.R. 1474. The mortgagee has the right to an order for possession of the property notwithstanding that there are counter allegations or a claim for set off by the mortgagee, no matter how serious, sound or unsound: *Midland Bank v. McGrath* [1996] E.G.C.S. 61 and *Ashley Guarantee plc v. Zacaria* [1993] 1 W.L.R. 62.
(3) Although there has been some suggestion in *Quennell v. Maltby* [1979] 1 All E.R. 568 that the right to possession is dependent on the mortgagor's default, subsequent cases have followed the traditional rule that a right to possession is a right and not a remedy.

KEY PRINCIPLE: *A mortgagee in possession is strictly accountable for any rents and profits received. The duty extends to obtaining the best rent if the property was managed with due diligence.*

White v. City of London Brewery Company 1889

The mortgagees of a public house, who took possession of the property, let it out with a restriction that the tenant should only take his supply of beer from the mortgagees.

HELD: (C.A.) The mortgagees had to account for such additional rent that it would have received if it had let the premises out without the restriction. (1889) 42 Ch. D. 237.

Section 36 of the Administration of Justice Act 1970 (as amended)

KEY PRINCIPLE: *Section 36 of the* Administration of Justice Act 1970 *as amended by section 8 of the* Administration of

Justice Act 1973, *authorises the court to suspend the order for possession or to postpone or adjourn the proceedings provided the mortgagor appears likely to be able to pay the sums due under the mortgage within a reasonable time.*

Target Home Loans Ltd v. Clothier 1994

The defendants charged their home as security for a loan. They stopped making monthly repayments in July 1990. In October 1991, the plaintiffs applied for an order for possession. This was adjourned for 56 days under section 36 of the *Administration of Justice Act 1970* (as amended). The plaintiffs appealed against this decision. Upon the defendants providing a bank draft of £10,000 and evidence of a prospective sale of the property, the proceedings were adjourned for four months. The plaintiffs again appealed against this order and the defendants made a small payment but produced evidence that they had placed the property on the market and the estate agents were optimistic of an early sale.

HELD: (C.A.) There was no evidence that the defendants could settle the sums due under the mortgage within a reasonable time. However, on the evidence available, the defendants would only be able to discharge the debt by a sale of the property and since an early sale would serve the interests of the parties, the court would defer the order for sale for three months. The plaintiffs would be entitled to possession if the defendants failed to settle the sums due within this time. [1994] 1 All E.R. 439.

COMMENTARY

In deciding whether to exercise its discretion to suspend or postpone the proceedings or order under section 36 of the *Administration of Justice Act 1970* as amended the court will have regard to the facts and circumstances of the case. In *Cheltenham and Gloucester Building Society v. Grant, The Times*, May 9, 1994, the Court of Appeal reiterated that the discretionary power under the *Administration of Justice Act 1970* could be exercised if the court was satisfied of the mortgagor's ability to pay the sums due under the mortgage within a reasonable time.

KEY PRINCIPLE: *The question of what amounts to a reasonable time for the purposes of section 36 of the* Administration of Justice Act 1970 *(as amended) is dependent on the circumstances of the case.*

Cheltenham and Gloucester Building Society v. Norgan 1996

In order to assist her husband's business, the defendant charged her home as security for a loan for the business. The repayments of the loan fell into arrears and the plaintiffs obtained for a possession order. This order was suspended twice but the arrears remained unpaid. The plaintiffs subsequently applied for a possession warrant which again was suspended twice to allow the defendant and her husband time to pay the arrears. As the arrears remained substantial the plaintiffs applied to issue the warrant but the defendant cross applied for a further suspension of the order. The judge at first instance granted the warrant for possession and the defendant appealed against this order.

HELD: (C.A.) When assessing what amounts to a reasonable period for the payment of mortgage arrears by the mortgagor, for the purposes of section 36 of the *Administration of Justice Act 1970* (as amended), it was appropriate for the court to take into account of the whole of the remaining part of the original term of the mortgage. The case was then remitted back to the County Court to determine whether it should exercise its discretion to suspend the warrant of possession. [1996] 1 All E.R. 449.

Bristol & West Building Society v. Ellis 1996

An initial order was granted where the second defendant was to pay £5,000 immediately and £200 per month thereafter. This was in addition to the interest payments to the Building Society. The possession order was suspended under the *Administration of Justice Act 1970*, on terms that she paid the £5,000 and discharged the mortgage debt by selling the property within three to five years, after the children had completed their education. The Building Society appealed on the ground that the period of repayment wasn't reasonable.

HELD: (C.A.) The concept of a reasonable period was not strictly definable. Ultimately, it depended on the circumstances of the case, having regard to the delay in selling the property which had already occurred and the adequacy of the security. However, on the facts of the case, there was insufficient evidence to show that the property could be sold at a sufficiently high price to discharge the debt within a three to five year period. As such the suspension order would be set aside and a possession order granted. *The Times*, May 2, 1996.

COMMENTARY

The effect of *Cheltenham and Gloucester Building Society v. Norgan* is that the court has the discretion under the 1970 Act to capitalise the arrears of mortgage payments and spread it over the remaining term of the mortgage, provided the circumstances of the case justified it. The difficulty with the case is that it would appear to allow substantial postponement of the order or proceedings for possession. Cases prior to this always assumed that the postponement would only be for a reasonably short duration to allow the mortgagor time to pay off the arrears. In *National & Provincial Building Society v. Lloyd* [1996] 1 All E.R. 630, a case decided shortly after *Norgan*, the Court of Appeal decided that if there was evidence of a proposed sale of property which had been mortgaged to the mortgagee, that is sufficient to justify the suspension of a possession order on the basis that it was likely that any sums due would be repaid within a reasonable period of time. These case are not in conflict as they relate to different issues. What is clear is that a reasonable period of time for the purposes of section 36 of the *Administration of Justice Act 1970* (as amended), is a question of fact dependent on the circumstances of each case.

[b] Mortgagee's power of sale

KEY PRINCIPLE: *Although the mortgagee is not a trustee of the power of sale, the mortgagee, in the exercise of its power of sale must, have regard to the interests of the mortgagor.*

Cuckmere Brick Co Ltd v. Mutual Finance Ltd 1971

The plaintiffs who owned land with planning permission to erect 100 flats charged it to the defendants as security for a loan. The plaintiff later obtained planning permission to erect 35 houses. Subsequently, the defendants' power of sale became exercisable and took possession of the land. In the advertisements for sale of the land by public auction, the planning permission to erect 35 houses was mentioned but not in respect of the 100 flats. The plaintiffs drew this to the defendants attention and requested that the auction be postponed. The defendants refused.

HELD: (C.A.) A mortgagee in the exercise of its power of sale owed a duty to the mortgagor to take reasonable care to obtain a proper price. The defendants were in breach of this duty in failing to adequately publicise the planning permission for the flats or in refusing to postpone the sale. [1971] 1 Ch. 949.

COMMENTARY
(1) Salmon L.J .suggested in that case that a mortgagee owes both the duty to act in good faith and the duty to take reasonable care to obtain the true market value (the other Lord Justices suggested that the duty is to obtain a proper price) of the mortgaged property at the moment that the mortgagee decides to sale. Thus, although the mortgagee is not a trustee of the power of sale, it owes the mortgagor a subjective duty of good faith and objective duty of reasonable care. Further, it has been decided in *Parker-Tweedale v. Dunbar Bank plc* (1991) 60 P. & C.R. 83, that a mortgagee in the exercise of its power of sale did not owe a duty of care independent to that owed to the mortgagor, to a person with a beneficial interest in the mortgaged property even though the mortgagee may have notice of such an interest.
(2) It should be noted that if the mortgagee is unaware of the existence of the planning permission affecting the mortgaged property, then no inference of breach of the duty to take reasonable care can be inferred: *Palmer v. Barclays Bank* (1972) 23 P. & C.R. 30.

KEY PRINCIPLE: *The mortgagee has a discretion to decide when to sell the mortgaged property in the exercise of its power of sale.*

China and South Sea Bank Ltd v. Tan Soon Gin 1990

The appellant creditor granted a loan to a company ("the debtor") which was secured by a guarantee from the respondent, who undertook to repay the sum advanced together with interest. It was also secured by a mortgage of shares of the debtor company, allegedly worth twice the loan amount. The debtor failed to repay the loan and although the shares were still worth more than the loan at that time, the appellant did not dispose of the shares in the exercise of its power of sale. After the shares had become worthless, the appellant brought an action against the surety demanding repayment of the loan and interest.

HELD: (P.C.) The appellant creditor owed no duty to the surety to exercise its power of sale with regards to the mortgaged shares. The appellant creditor could decide in its own interest whether and when to sell the property. The surety was therefore liable to repay the amount outstanding. [1990] 1 A.C. 536.

COMMENTARY
In the earlier case of *Standard Chartered Bank v. Walker* [1982] 1 W.L.R. 1410, Lord Denning suggested that part of the mortgagee's duty to take reasonable care in obtaining a proper price on the sale of the mortgaged property, may include the duty to choose an appropriate time for the sale. However, *China and South Sea Bank Ltd v. Tan Soon Gin* makes it clear that although there is a duty on the mortgagee to obtain the current market value, the mortgagee nonetheless has the discretion to decide if and when he should sell.

KEY PRINCIPLE: *A purported sale of the mortgaged property by the mortgagee to itself or its servant is void and ineffective although the sale may be at market value.*

Martinson v. Clowes 1882
The Building Society was the mortgagee of five houses which it was selling under a power of sale. Before the properties were auctioned, part of it was sold by private contract. The remainder of the properties were offered for sale by auction. The secretary of the Building Society bid for a number of the properties, who eventually became the owner of two of the properties.

HELD: (Ch.D.) A mortgagee exercising its power of sale cannot purchase the property on its own account and likewise neither can an agent of the mortgagee do so. Accordingly, the sale of the two properties to the secretary of the Building Society would be set aside. (1882) 21 Ch. D. 857.

COMMENTARY

Where there is a sale of the mortgaged property to the mortgagee or its agent or servant, the sale is likely to set aside because of the potential conflict of interest. In the case of a sale of the mortgaged property to an associated person or company, the burden of proof is on the mortgagee to establish that the sale was in good faith and that it had taken reasonable precautions to obtain the best price obtainable at the time: *Tse Kwong Lam v. Wong Chit Sen* [1983] 1 W.L.R. 1349.

KEY PRINCIPLE: *"The money which is received by the mortgagee, arising from the sale, after discharge of prior encumbrances . . . shall be held by him in trust to be applied . . . first, in payment of all costs, charges and expenses properly incurred by him as incident to the sale . . . and secondly in discharge of the mortgage money, interest, and costs . . . and the residue of the money so received shall be paid to the person entitled to the mortgaged property . . ."* Section 105 Law of Property Act 1925.

Halifax Building Society v. Thomas 1995

Thomas had a mortgage with the Halifax Building Society. Upon default of payments, the Building Society took possession and exercised its power of sale. After the payment of the loan, interests and costs, the Building Society placed the surplus in a suspense account. The Building Society claimed it was entitled to keep the surplus on the basis that it wouldn't have arisen had it not granted the loan to Thomas.

HELD: (C.A.) The mortgage was only the security for the loan and section 105 of the *Law of Property Act 1925* was clear as to the mortgagee's duty with respect to the proceeds of sale. The surplus was therefore held on trust for Thomas.[1995] 4 All E.R. 673.

COMMENTARY

The case serves as a useful reminder that section 105 of the *Law of Property Act 1925* is clear as to the application of the proceeds of sale, and that the mortgage is merely a security for the loan.

Section 91(2) of the
Law of Property Act 1925

KEY PRINCIPLE: *Where the mortgagor wishes to sell the mortgaged property but the mortgagee refuses to consent to the sale, the court has the power under section 91(2) of the* Law of Property Act 1925 *to grant an order for the sale of the property.*

Palk v. Mortgage Services Funding plc 1993

The plaintiff mortgagors were unable to pay the instalments under a mortgage and secured a buyer for the mortgaged property for £283,000. The amount needed to redeem the mortgage was £358,587. The mortgagee refused to consent to the sale but obtained an order for possession of the property with a view of leasing out the property and postponing the sale till a later date. The rental income would not have been sufficient to pay the interest due under the loan. The plaintiffs applied for an order for sale under section 91(2) of the *Law of Property Act 1925*.

HELD: (C.A.) The court in deciding whether to exercise its discretion under section 91(2) of the 1925 Act would have regard to the interests of the parties concerned. In the circumstances of the case, it was just and equitable to grant an order for the sale of the property notwithstanding that the proceeds of sale would not have been enough to pay off the loan. [1993] Ch. 330.

COMMENTARY
It was made clear in this case that the court's discretion under section 91(2) of the *Law of Property Act 1925* is unfettered and that it could grant an order for sale of the mortgaged property even in cases of "negative equity."

KEY PRINCIPLE: *Section 36 of the* Administration of Justice Act 1970 *(as amended) cannot be used to suspend possession proceedings or orders so that an application can be made by the mortgagor for an order for sale under section 91(2) of the* Law or Property Act 1925 *in cases of negative equity.*

Cheltenham and Gloucester plc v. Krausz 1996

The plaintiff mortgagee obtained a possession order against the defendant mortgagor. Subsequently, the defendant found a buyer for the property. However, the plaintiff refused consent to the sale because of negative equity and also because it believed that a higher price could be obtained for the property. The defendants made an application under section 36 of the *Administration of Justice Act 1970* to postpone the possession order as well as an order for sale of the property under section 91 of the *Law of Property Act 1925*.

HELD: (C.A.) Section 36 of the *Administration of Justice Act 1970* could not be used to postpone a mortgagee's possession of the property so that the mortgagor could make an application for an order of sale under section 91 of the *Law of Property Act 1925*. This was especially so if the proceeds of such a sale was insufficient to pay off the amount due to the mortgagee. *The Times*, November 20, 1996.

COMMENTARY

The relationship between section 91 of the *Law of Property Act 1925* and section 36 of the *Administration of Justice Act 1970* (as amended) is that an application to postpone the possession order and an application for an order for sale by the mortgagor will not succeed where the proceeds of sale is insufficient to repay the loan. This puts a limitation on *Palk v. Mortgage Services Funding plc*.

Mortgages of Equitable Interests—The Rule in Dearle v. Hall

KEY PRINCIPLE: *Unless notice is given to the holders of the legal estate, mortgages of equitable interests will not have priority.*

Dearle v. Hall 1823

Brown was given a life interest in a fund, the income which amounted to about £93 a year, by his father through the latter's will. Brown subsequently granted two annuities which was charged upon and payable out of his life interest. The first annuity amounted to £37 and was granted to William Dearle and the second amounted to £27 which was granted to Caleb

Sherring. Brown then sold his life interest in the fund to Joseph Hall. Joseph Hall's solicitors made proper enquiries but had no notice of the two annuities. The solicitors gave notice to the executors of Brown's father's will of the transfer of the life interest from Brown to Joseph Hall. The executors subsequently discovered the existence of the annuities. William Dearle and Caleb Sherring claimed that their interest took priority over Joseph Hall's interest.

HELD: (Ch.D.) Joseph Hall's interest took priority over the annuities granted to William Dearle and Caleb Sherring. This was because the equitable rule that the first in time prevails did not apply in the context of the legal estate. For the annuities to bind the legal estate, notice had to be given to the holders of the legal estate, which in this case were the executors. This had not been done and therefore the annuities did not have priority over Joseph Hall's interest. (1823–28) 3 Russ. 1.

COMMENTARY

(1) In summary, the rule in *Dearle v. Hall* is that the mortgage of an equitable interest will have priority from the time written notice is given to the legal owners. In *Dearle v. Hall*, Joseph Hall's interest had priority over the annuities because his solicitors had given notice of the transfer of the life interest from Brown to him, to the executors of the father's estate who held the legal title to it.

(2) It should also be noted that the rule in *Dearle v. Hall* appears to apply to both registered and unregistered land as well.

---

9. EASEMENTS

Basic Requirements

KEY PRINCIPLE: *The four requisite characteristics of an easement are: there must be a dominant and servient tenement; an easement must "accommodate" the dominant tenement; dominant and servient owners must be different persons; and a right over land cannot amount to an easement, unless it is capable of forming the subject matter of a grant.*

In Re Ellenborough Park 1956

The vendors sold plots surrounding Ellenborough Park. The conveyances granted purchasers "full enjoyment of the pleasure ground". This enjoyment was to be held in common with other persons granted "such easements" and was subject to payment of a fair proportion of the cost of keeping the park in good order. The vendor covenanted with purchasers and successors to keep the park as a pleasure ground.

HELD: (C.A.) "Full enjoyment of the pleasure ground" was a common and clearly understood concept. The right of enjoyment accommodated the dominant tenement even if there was no absolute necessary connection between enjoyment of the park and the premises. The rights granted and obligations incurred were not repugnant to the freeholder's proprietorship or possession of the park. The right to use the pleasure ground was beneficial to the houses and was not merely a right of recreation and amusement. [1956] Ch. 131.

COMMENTARY

The case is used as authority for the four characteristics of an easement. The court adopted as correct the formulations set out in Cheshire's *Modern Real Property* (7th edn., pp. 456). The first and third requirements were not problematic here. The court found the first satisfied notwithstanding that enjoyment of the park could benefit people unconnected to the neighbouring premises. The court found the concept of enjoyment of the park sufficiently certain to be the subject matter of a grant. In modern terms it is clear that such a right adds to the use and value to the land and can be easily regarded as an easement.

There Must be a Dominant and Servient Tenement

KEY PRINCIPLE: *There must be a dominant and servient tenement which must be defined at the time of the grant.*

London & Blenheim Estates Ltd v. Ladbroke Retail Parks Ltd 1994

The plaintiff bought land together with an easement of car parking over land retained by the vendor. The schedule to the sale agreement allowed for unspecified later acquired land to be benefited by the easement.

HELD: (C.A.) For an easement to exist the dominant tenement must exist and be defined at the time of grant of the easement. The easement could not therefore benefit the after-acquired land which was unknown at the time of the grant of the easement. [1994] 1 W.L.R. 31.

COMMENTARY
An easement cannot exist "in gross", that is, exist without benefiting a known piece of land. Easements can be distinguished from public rights of way in that the latter are enjoyed without reference to benefited land and are hence not property rights.

The Easement Must Accommodate the Dominant Tenement

KEY PRINCIPLE: *A right conferring a personal benefit does not accommodate the dominant tenement unless it also benefits the land as land.*

Hill v. Tupper 1863
Under his lease the plaintiff claimed the sole right of letting out pleasure boats for hire upon the adjacent canal.

HELD: (Exch) The right did not accommodate the tenement but was a personal licence to him. (1863) 2 H. & C. 121.

COMMENTARY
The case may well be differently decided nowadays on the basis that mooring rights are valuable and would benefit any owner of the land not just one who used them for business. The plaintiff may have had a contractual claim against the canal owners but the court were unwilling to infer a property right against a third party. Compare this with *Moody v. Steggles* (1879) 12 Ch. D. 261, where the right to place a sign for a public house on another's land was held to be capable of being an easement. Here, the benefited land had been used as a pub for more than 200 years. The court found that the land and its use had become inextricably linked so that the right was not a personal commercial benefit, but something

which benefited that land itself. To accommodate the dominant tenement:

[i]   the right should benefit the land as land;
[ii]   the land should be adjacent or close enough to identifiably benefit;
[iii] the right should add value or use to the land;
[iv] the right must confer more than a personal benefit to the current owner.

Dominant and Servient Owners Must be Different Persons

KEY PRINCIPLE: *An easement cannot be enjoyed against oneself.*

Kilgour v. Gaddes 1904

The defendant claimed as a defence to the plaintiff's trespass action that he had acquired a prescriptive right to use the well on the plaintiff's land. Both plaintiff and defendant were tenants of the same landlord.

HELD: (C.A.) An easement could not be acquired by prescription by one tenant against another tenant of the same landlord. [1904] 1 K.B. 457.

COMMENTARY
Such a usage could be a leasehold term or a licence but could not be an easement as the freeholder cannot enjoy a right against himself in relation to one part of his land against another. It has subsequently been held that such usages may convert to easements upon the conveyance of part of the land. See *Wheeldon v. Burrows* and *Wright v. MacAdam* below.

The Easement Must Form the Subject Matter of a Grant

KEY PRINCIPLE: *The right must be a recognised one made by a capable grantor to a capable grantee.*

Phipps v. Pears 1965

The defendant demolished his house exposing his neighbour's flank wall to the weather. The houses had not been joined but were close enough so that the plaintiff's house had been shielded from the weather and was not otherwise protected.

HELD: (C.A.) There was no known easement to be protected from the weather. The plaintiff had no claim to stop the defendant demolishing his house exposing the plaintiff's house to the weather. [1965] 1 Q.B. 76.

COMMENTARY

(1) In *Sedgewick Forbes Bland Payne Group v. Regional Properties* (1979) 257 E.G. 64, it was indicated that an easement of protection may be possible in relation to a property above another.

(2) The standard recognized easements include rights of passage, water, air and light. A right to a specially high degree of light for the benefit of a greenhouse can be acquired: *Allen v. Greenwood* [1980] Ch. 119.

(3) Slightly anomalous but recognised easements are those of:

Support: Had the houses in the present case been attached to each other, the plaintiff may have been able to claim an easement of support. The easement of support prevents the servient owner from demolishing his side (*Dalton v. Angus* (1881) 6 App. Cas.740) but doesn't require the servient owner to maintain it so that it doesn't collapse through disrepair (see *Jones v. Pritchard*, below).

Fencing: The easement of fencing (*Crow v. Wood* [1971] Q.B. 77) obliges the servient owner to maintain fencing. This is unusual in that it falls foul of the normal requirement that the servient owner shouldn't be burdened by expense in observing an easement's obligation.

Storage: The easement of storage could be seen as being more in the nature of a lease or licence but can fall into the domain of easements provided it is defined with certainty (*Wright v. MacAdam*, below) and doesn't serve to exclude the servient owner of the proper right of possession of his own land (*Copeland v. Greenhalf*, below).

Usage of facilities: The easement of using facilities could likewise be associated with other kinds of rights but has been accepted in relation to using facilities such as a lavatory (*Miller v. Emcer Products Ltd* [1956] Ch. 304), a kitchen

(*Heywood. v. Mallalieu* (1883) 25 Ch. 357) or a post box
(*Goldberg v. Edwards* [1950] Ch. 247).

KEY PRINCIPLE: *An easement must be defined with
certainty.*

Trailfinders Ltd v. Razuki 1988

The plaintiff granted the defendants a lease of neighbouring
land reserving the right of passage of pipes, wires and other
conduits for, amongst other things, electric current. The plaintiff later sought to pass computer cables across the land.

HELD: (Ch.D.) The right reserved did not extend to entering
the premises and laying computer cables which were said to be
"of an entirely novel kind." [1988] 2 E.G.L.R.46.

COMMENTARY
(1) Generally rights of passage must be along specific channels. Rights of air should be along specific routes such as air
ducts (*Wong v. Beaumont Property Trust Ltd*, below) not
generally across the surface (*Harris v. De Pinna* (1886) 33
Ch.D. 238) or a draught across chimneys (*Bryant v. Lefever*
(1879 4 C.P.D. 172).
(2) Rights of light should be for light coming through defined
apertures not a general right to light coming across the land
(*Colls v. Home & Colonial Stores Ltd* [1904] A.C. 179).
(3) Rights of water should be through particular channels or
pipes (*Race v. Ward* (1855) 4 El & Bl 702); there is no general
right to water percolating through the soil.
(4) Rights of way should be across a given route. They may
enjoy incidental benefits such as unloading and the right to
repair or improve the route. The present and reasonably foreseeable purposes should not be exceeded; the form of use
can, however, change. A right of way cannot be extended to
include a right to store equipment (*VT Engineering Co Ltd v.
Richard Barland & Co Ltd* (1968) 19 P. & C.R. 890) but its
form of use can be changed from, for example, horse drawn
vehicles to motor vehicles (*Sunset Properties Pty Ltd v.
Johnston* (1975) 3 B.P.R. 9185).

Factors in Claims to Easements

KEY PRINCIPLE: *A grantor may not derogate from grant.*

Cable v. Bryant 1908

The plaintiff leased a stable from the defendant who subsequently put up a hoarding blocking ventilation to the stable.

HELD: The defendant could not derogate from grant by making the stable unusable. A claim to an easement of air through a defined aperture was recognized notwithstanding that there was no defined air-flow channel through the servient land.[1908] 1 Ch. 259.

COMMENTARY
(1) In most cases a defined air-flow channel is required (*Bryant v. Lefever*). The court may have been willing to vary this requirement in order to emphasize the principle of non-derogation from grant.
(2) Lessors' reservations of easements are likely to be construed strictly against the lessor on the basis that to seek to extend the reservation later would be to derogate from the grant of the lease (*Trailfinders Ltd v. Razuki*, above).

KEY PRINCIPLE: *An easement should not have the effect of excluding the servient owner from possession of his property by giving the claimant exclusive or joint use.*

Copeland v. Greenhalf 1952

The defendant claimed by 50 years' long use a prescriptive right to store vehicles on a strip of land which the plaintiff used for access between her house and orchard. The vehicles were stored at the strip of land's narrowest point which was just 15 feet wide.

HELD: (Ch.D.) The right claimed would not be accepted as an easement as it would effectively give the whole beneficial use of the strip of land to the defendant.[1952] Ch. 488.

COMMENTARY
(1) A claim to exclusive use or joint use will usually fail. In cases involving use of facilities greater leeway seems to be afforded claimants presumably on the basis that use of a lavatory (*Miller v. Emcer Products Ltd*, above) or a kitchen

for washing (*Heywood v. Mallialieu*, above) would only be for limited parts of a day in the same way as passing along a right of way is a limited use of the land. The right to store coal in a garden shed (*Wright v. MacAdam*, below) is perhaps more difficult to justify. In *Grigsby v. Melville* [1973] 1 All E.R. 385 it was held that a claim for an easement of storage in a cellar would fail as it amounted to a claim for exclusive use.

(2) It should be remembered that an easement of car parking is recognised as an easement provided it does not exclude the use of it by the servient owner and is defined with certainty: *London & Blenheim Estates Ltd. v. Ladbroke Retail Parks Ltd*, above.

KEY PRINCIPLE: *An easement should not involve expenditure or any positive obligation by the servient owner.*

Regis Property v. Redman 1956

A lease contained a covenant to supply hot water and central heating.

HELD: (Q.B.D.) The right to this benefit was not in the nature of a property right of an easement. [1956] 2 Q.B. 612.

COMMENTARY
The easement of fencing (*Crow v. Wood* [1971] Q.B. 77) is an acknowledged exception where expense is imposed on servient owners fixed with an obligation to maintain fencing. In *Liverpool City Council v. Irwin* [1977] A.C. 239 the use of stairs, lifts and rubbish chutes were held to be implied easements. Inevitably, maintenance of these would involve expense which the court may have felt legitimate in the context of a public authority landlord. The terms of the lease were inadequate and the court used this artifice to give the lease its proper effect, though it might have been easier to phrase the obligations as implied leasehold terms rather than implied easements.

(2) An easement should not require the owner to carry out positive acts in order to respect them. This is often coincident with the tests that the servient owner should not incur expense or have to give permission. It is sometimes said that the courts will not accept new negative easements. This is perhaps an overstatement of the principle that a court will not accept new easements which exclude the servient

owner from the proper possession of his property. Whether an easement is positive or negative in character does not depend on how it is phrased, but on the content of the obligation. It could be said that if the servient owner can respect an easement by doing nothing then it is a negative easement.

KEY PRINCIPLE: *An easement should be in the nature of a right not a permission.*

Green v. Ashco Horticulturist Ltd 1966

The plaintiff was a lessee of a shop. The original lease was granted in 1931 and renewed in 1959. The defendant owned the freehold of the shop and other property, including a passageway from the street past a courtyard behind the shop and onto some garages. In 1963, the plaintiff claimed that he had a right of way along the passageway having used this since 1931 as sole means of access to the courtyard. He alleged that this right was being blocked. On evidence, it was found that until 1960 there had been gates between the passageway and courtyard which was only open during office hours. There had been times when the plaintiff had not been allowed to use the passageway at all. The lease also allowed the lessor unlimited power to build on the land.

HELD: (Ch.D.) That the use of the passageway was by permission and not as of right and therefore could not be claimed against the freeholder as an easement. [1966] 1 W.L.R. 889.

COMMENTARY
In *Burrows v. Lang* [1901] 2 Ch. 502, a claim to take water from an artificial water source was rejected as it would depend on the servient owner giving intermittent permission by refilling the source. See also *Gardner v. Hodgson's Kingston Brewery* below.

Acquisition of Easements

KEY PRINCIPLE: *An easement can arise by necessity.*

Nickerson v. Barraclough 1980

The plaintiff bought a field. It was landlocked except for a lane which ran parallel to the field and continued onto a public highway. The lane was accessed by a bridge from the plaintiff's land over a ditchap. The 1906 conveyance of most of what became the plaintiff's land contained a restriction that the vendor did not undertake to make up any roads nor did he grant any rights of way. A 1922 conveyance of a strip of land brought together what was now the plaintiff's land. The 1973 conveyance was expressed to include a right of way over the lane insofar as the vendor had power to convey it. The defendant knocked down the bridge over the ditch to the lane twice and denied the easement of a right of way.

HELD: (C.A.) As a matter of public policy no transaction should without good reason be regarded as depriving access to the land conveyed. The 1906 conveyance freed the vendor from any obligation to make up roads but did not preclude an easement of necessity from arising. [1980] Ch. 325.

COMMENTARY
An easement of way for agricultural and sporting purposes to land beyond that conveyed in the 1922 conveyance was also held to have arisen by virtue of section 62 of the *Law of Property Act 1925*. In *Corporation of London v. Riggs* (1880) 13 Ch. D. 798, it was held that a right of way of necessity is limited to what is necessary at the time of the grant. Thus, access to the land for agricultural purposes cannot later be extended to access for building purposes.

KEY PRINCIPLE: *An easement can come about by the intention of the parties.*

Wong v. Beaumont Property Trust Ltd 1965
A lease of cellar premises for use as a restaurant was conveyed with a stipulation that the lessee would comply with health regulations. These included ventilation. The new landlords refused permission for the erection of a ventilation duct fixed to the building above which they retained.

HELD: (C.A.) There was an easement of necessity to erect and maintain a ventilation duct.[1965] 1 Q.B. 173.

COMMENTARY
This case is often cited as supporting the principle that an easement can arise from the intention of the parties. The Court of Appeal did, however, characterize it as an easement of necessity. In fact neither party realised where the air duct

would subsequently have to be. It is fair to say, however, that the intended use of the premises made the easement a necessity which it would not otherwise have been.

KEY PRINCIPLE: *An easement of intention can arise if there is a common intention as to the purpose and manner of use of the land and that an easement is necessary to give effect to that use.*

Stafford v. Lee 1992

An area of woodland was conveyed described as fronting a road but without expressly granting a right over it. The plaintiff subsequently built a dwelling on the woodland. The defendants conceded a right of way but only for purposes necessary for the reasonable enjoyment of the land as woodland.

HELD: (C.A.) The question was whether the parties at the time of the conveyance intended the land to be used in a definite and particular manner, not how the land was in fact used at the time of the grant. The plans which accompanied the grant indicated that the parties intended that the land be developed for residential purposes. *The Times.* November 16, 1992.

COMMENTARY
Intention is again defined in terms of what is necessary to achieve the intention of the parties as opposed to what is objectively necessary.

KEY PRINCIPLE: *A grant of a part of a tenement passes with it those continuous and apparent "easements" over the other part of the land which are necessary for the enjoyment of the granted land which have hitherto been in use.*

Wheeldon v. Burrows 1879

A workshop and adjoining piece of land owned by the same vendor were put up for sale. The land was sold and the workshop retained but later sold to a different purchaser. The workshop had windows which received light from the piece of land previously sold.

HELD: (Ch.D.) There was no reservation of light made when the land was sold. No right to light could therefore pass to the subsequent owner of the workshop. (1879) 12 Ch. 31.

COMMENTARY

Courts are unwilling to allow implied reservations of easements except where the easement is of clear necessity. To allow implied reservation would be to allow derogation from grant. The case is perhaps more important for the effect it could have on the converse facts. If the vendor sold the workshop first and retained the other piece of land the purchaser would have the benefit of an easement of light provided its existence had been continuous, apparent and necessary for the reasonable enjoyment of the land as well as being in use at the time of the sale. This could be binding on subsequent owners of the land.

The rule in *Wheeldon v. Burrows* is problematic. The passage of the easement upon the grant of the land cannot be correct as prior to the grant there could have been no existing prior easement because both the workshop and piece of land lay within the ownership and occupation of the same person. One of the four essential requirements for an easement is that the dominant and servient owners are different persons. The best that could have existed before the grant is what has come to be known as a "quasi easement." These can be converted to an easement if the conditions set out in the case are met. In *Borman v. Griffith* [1930] 1 Ch. 493 it was held that an easement of a right of way could be implied into a specifically enforceable agreement for a lease under the *Wheeldon v. Burrows* rule (even when the usage was regular if not continuous). In *Ward v. Kirkland* [1967] Ch. 194 the claim to a right to enter neighbour's land to maintain a wall failed on the ground that there was no apparent evidence manifesting the exercise of such a right.

KEY PRINCIPLE: *An easement can come into existence as a result of section 62 of the Law of Property Act 1925.*

Wright v. Macadam 1949

A tenant was allowed by the defendant landlord to use the garden shed for the storage of coal. After three years, in 1943 the landlord granted the plaintiffs a new one-year lease of the property plus an extra room. The plaintiffs continued to use the shed though there was never any written agreement to this effect. Four years later the landlord asked for an extra charge for the use of the shed. The plaintiffs refused and the landlord removed the shed.

HELD: (C.A.) The use of the shed was a recognized right in land. This right passed with the agreement of 1943. That agreement was a conveyance of land and by virtue of section 62 *Law of Property Act 1925* a conveyance is deemed to pass with it, *inter alia*, all rights and easements unless expressly excluded. [1949] 2 K.B. 744.

COMMENTARY
Like *Wheeldon v. Burrows* there is a logical problem that the conveyance is being used to change something into an ease-ment which previously may have been regarded as merely a leasehold covenant or a licence. The purpose of section 62 is not to create new land rights but to save words in con-veyances. However, there is also a similarity in the cases in that it may have been unjust to allow the landlord to effectively derogate from grant. In *Graham v. Philcox* [1948] Q.B. 747, a right of way benefited a lease of a flat. The lease was subse-quently conveyed to new lessees. When that flat was enlarged with the neighbouring flat into a single residence the question arose as to whether the right of way was co-terminus with the lease. It was held that a subsequent lease was a conveyance which by the effect of section 62 created an easement. The enlargement into a single dwelling did not deny that creation of an easement. Again, it is arguable that the right of way should have been regarded as a leasehold term only.

KEY PRINCIPLE: *For section 62 to operate so as to convert some right into an easement there must have been diversity of ownership or occupation under which the* de facto *"right" was enjoyed.*

Long v. Gowlett 1923
The vendor owned two plots of land along a river. He had passed from one to the other to clear blockages from the river. The purchaser of one plot claimed this right over the purchaser of the other.

HELD: (Ch.D.) The precursor to section 62 could not pass such a right unless there had been some prior, even precarious, right over land owned or occupied by another.

Sovmots Investments v. Secretary of State for the Environment 1979

In 1960 the Greater London Council leased a site to the first plaintiffs for 150 years. They developed it, building maisonettes on top of showrooms and garages. The maisonettes were not occupied. In 1972 Camden Borough Council made a compulsory purchase order of the lease of the maisonettes. They documented (outside the Order itself) certain ancillary rights such as those of support from the building below and rights of passage of electricity water etc. which they regarded as passing under section 62. In 1974 the first plaintiffs sub-let the maisonettes to the second plaintiffs. The plaintiffs appealed that the ancillary rights could not pass by virtue of section 62.

HELD: (H.L.) The ancillary rights claimed did not pass as there had not been diversity of ownership or occupation of the quasi-dominant and quasi-servient tenements.[1979] A.C. 144.

COMMENTARY
(1) The notion that diversity of occupation less than diversity of ownership is sufficient still leaves a problem that a usage enjoyed in a leasehold or licence context could be converted to a right, claimed as between freeholders.
(2) In *Sovmots Investments v. Secretary of State for the Environment*, in analysing the definitions of house, appurtenance and land, the House of Lords also found that the ancillary rights could not be claimed unless they pre-existed with clear definition. There appears to be an underlying dispute as to who should have effective control over the property, the developers or the Borough Council, and to the appropriateness of the Council using compulsory purchase orders as a part of its function of providing housing.

KEY PRINCIPLE: *To acquire an easement by prescription, the use must be as of right.*

Gardner v. Hodgson's Kingston Brewery 1903

For more than forty years a landowner crossed his neighbour's yard to reach the public road from his own yard. This was done in return for an annual payment. There was no written agreement and insufficient evidence as to the origin of the agreement or payment.

HELD: (H.L.) The payment was for the use of the access way and that usage was thus not as of right. Given the usage was on evidence not as of right the presumption of a lost modern grant under the *Prescription Act 1832* could not be made. [1903] A.C. 229.

COMMENTARY
Long user cannot make for a prescriptive right if there is no property right underlying the usage. In this case the use of an access way took the form of a licence. The traditional phrasing of the requirement is that the use must be *nec vi, nec clam, nec precario*, that is, not by force, not secretly, and not with permission.

KEY PRINCIPLE: *Acquiescence does not equate to permission.*

Mills v. Silver 1991
The defendants bought a hill farm, the only vehicular access to which was over a track across the plaintiff's land. The previous owner had used the track openly, without force and without permission albeit not frequently between 1922 and 1981. The track was only passable in dry weather. The defendants arranged to lay a stone road to make the track passable in all weather. The plaintiff sought an injunction and damages for trespass.

HELD: (C.A.) The previous use of the track had to be sufficient to warrant the implication of a lost modern grant. The use was open and toleration of its use did not rebut the presumption of a grant. The user was as of right known about and acquiesced to by the servient owners.[1991] Ch. 271.

COMMENTARY
The acquiescence is in effect regarded as evidence of the grant of right rather than permission denying the right. (Compare with *Jones v. Price* [1965] 2 Q.B. 618, where use of a track to drive sheep was held on evidence to be based on original and ongoing permission, rather than grant followed by

use as of right. Relevant evidence included the fact that similar permission was given to others.). That the farm was otherwise landlocked may have been an underlying consideration. The defendants were, however, held to be trespassing in relation to improving the track. The grant of an easement allows for maintaining its usability but not improving it. The improvements increased the burden on the servient owner. By holding that there was a trespass, the court recognized the easement to the extent that it existed when the hill farm was bought. The damages paid for the trespass done in improving reflect the extra burden imposed on the servient owner. See *Trailfinders Ltd v. Razuki* above as to extending easements.

KEY PRINCIPLE: *To acquire an easement by prescription the period of use must be 20 years without interruption.*

Reilly v. Orange 1955

In September 1934 the plaintiff granted his neighbour, the defendant, permission to use his driveway for domestic purposes. In December 1953 the plaintiff withdrew that permission and in July 1954 brought an action in court to determine the land's use. The defendant claimed an easement by prescription.

HELD: (C.A.) An easement by way of prescription required a full 20 years' use without interruption. Section 4 of the *Prescription Act 1832* deems that period to be the period next before the commencement of an action of a matter relating to the period. The defendants claim therefore failed. [1955] 2 Q.B. 112.

COMMENTARY
(1) Where there is an interruption, it must be acquiesced to for one year in order to be effective. Here, the defendant claimed that the bringing of the action was an interruption which could not be acquiesced to for one full year before the completion of 20 years. The defendant then argued that it could not therefore be an effective interruption against him and that his claim to a prescriptive easement was good. Ingenious as this argument was, the court held that the bringing of the action was not an interruption for the purposes of the Act but a defining event against which the previous 20-year period should be calculated.
(2) In *Newnham v. Willison* (1987) 56 P.&C.R. 8, the plaintiff

had a right of way over a driveway which merged into a track. The plaintiff argued that the turning was from one to the other was a swept curve, the defendant said it was a sharp corner and placed a post at the junction to enforce that view. The post was place in about March 1983, the plaintiff brought his action in June 1984. The Court of Appeal held that there had been an interruption for more than a year in the 20 years preceding the action so that there was no prescriptive right to use the swept curve.

KEY PRINCIPLES:

[i] *To acquire a prescriptive right at common law there must be use since time immemorial. There is a presumption of this if there has been 20 years uninterrupted use. The presumption is rebutted upon proof that the right began after 1189 or the land was in common ownership since 1189.*

[ii] *To acquire an easement by lost modern grant there must be 20 years uninterrupted use. This raises a presumption of a lost modern grant which can be rebutted by proof that the grant was impossible.*

[iii] *To acquire a prescriptive right under the Prescription Act 1832 the usage must be uninterrupted in the relevant period leading up to the action.*

Tehidy Minerals v. Norman 1971

The defendant farmers claimed rights of common of grazing over a down owned by the plaintiff. Some of the farms had been in common ownership with the down until purchased by the defendant in 1920. In 1941 the down was requisitioned by the Ministry of Agriculture and Fisheries. In 1954 the Ministry granted the commoners' association, including all defendants, a licence to use the down for grazing. After derequisition the association paid the plaintiff for permission to control grazing on the down.

To assert control over the down the plaintiff erected a fence across the middle of the down. The defendants dismantled the fence and were consequently sued for trespass. The defendants claimed that they had acquired rights of common of grazing over the down at common law, by lost modern grant and under the *Prescription Act 1832*.

HELD: (C.A.) The period of requisition had displaced all other interests in the property during that period, so that the claim to rights of common of grazing over the down failed under the Prescription Act. There had not been 20 years' uninterrupted use immediately prior to the action being brought. However, it is still possible to ask if rights have been acquired by common law prescription or the doctrine of lost modern grant.

In relation to those farms not previously in common ownership with the down there was proof of a period of 20 years' enjoyment of a profit raising a presumption of use since time immemorial. That presumption was not rebutted, so the right existed by common law prescription.

In relation to the farms in common ownership there was proof of 20 years' enjoyment from 1920 to 1941 raising a presumption of a lost modern grant. That presumption was not rebutted so the right existed by the doctrine of lost modern grant. Common law prescription would not help in relation to this land as the presumption of use since time immemorial was rebutted by the land being in common ownership before 1921. [1971] 2 Q.B. 528.

COMMENTARY
The case illustrates the inconsistency whereby a prescriptive right can be rejected by one method but accepted by another.

KEY PRINCIPLE: *The doctrine of lost modern grant survives as a legal fiction whereby an easement can be deemed to have been created.*

Bridle v. Ruby 1989
In the conveyance of a plot of land there was a reservation of an easement over a driveway but this had not been agreed and was crossed out. The successors in title used the driveway in the mistaken belief that they had the right to do so.

HELD: (C.A.) That the driveway was used under a mistaken belief as to the grant of an easement did not rebut the presumption of a lost modern grant. [1989] Q.B. 169.

COMMENTARY

It had been thought that the doctrine of lost modern grant was rendered unnecessary by the *Prescription Act 1832*. The inadequacies of the Act, however, allowed for the doctrine's return. This case illustrates the strength of the presumption which appears to survive even proof that there was no grant. The legal fiction of a grant after its apparent denial prevailed because there clearly was 20 years' use.

Extinguishment of Easements

Easements can be extinguished where the dominant and servient tenement come into the same ownership and occupation. During unity of possession the rights will be suspended. Easements are also extinguished by release which can be express or implied by abandonment.

KEY PRINCIPLE: *Abandonment must be supported by evidence that the dominant owner and his successors do not intend to use the easement again.*

Benn v. Hardinge 1992

A track ran along the boundary of the appellant's land connecting the entrances to two of his fields. In 1818 an enclosure order made the track into a private pathway benefiting amongst others the owners of the appellants land. Neither the appellant or his predecessors used the track as they had alternative access. The appellant now wished to use the pathway when other parts of his land became waterlogged.

HELD: (C.A.) The setting out of the private carriageway necessarily created a right of way as there could have been no purpose in setting it out for the appellant's predecessor unless it was for the right to use it. The fact that no one had cause to use the track did not of itself raise a presumption of abandonment even after 175 years. (1992) 66 P. & C.R. 246.

Liability to Repair

KEY PRINCIPLE: *A dominant owner is not liable for damage caused by the proper use of an easement.*

Jones v. Pritchard 1908

The defendants house was built with a party wall connecting it to the plaintiffs house. It was agreed that the ownership be divided along a vertical plane which bisected the chimney flues serving both properties. The flues on the defendant's side became defective due to subsidence. Use of the flues then resulted in smoke escaping through cracks, entering the plaintiff's house and causing damage.

HELD: (Ch.D.) There was an implied mutual grant of right to use the flues. The defendant was not liable for damage caused by use of the easement. The use was as contemplated by the parties and was not negligent. [1908] 1 Ch. 630.

COMMENTARY

(1) A servient owner is not bound to carry out repairs. Generally positive obligations are not consistent with easements. The servient owner could not destroy the supporting wall but could not be required to maintain it. Either party could carry out repairs on their own side and could gain reasonable access to effect repairs on the other side.

(2) In *Leakey v. National Trust for Places of Historic Interest or Natural Beauty* [1980] Q.B. 485 the House of Lords held that an occupier had a general duty in relation to hazards occurring on his land affecting his neighbour. The occupier was held liable for damage caused by the natural slippage of earth. Where damage was foreseeable the occupier should take reasonable care to avoid that damage. This case, however, says more about general occupiers' duties than it does about liabilities of servient owners. Similarly in *Bradburn v. Lindsay* [1983] 3 All E.R. 468, principles of negligence and nuisance prevailed over traditional views as to the content of the obligation in an easement of support. There it was held that a landowner was liable to the neighbour caused by negligence in allowing such disrepair that a demolition order became necessary thus removing the support to the neighbour's property.

Protection of easements

Before the system of land registration was introduced, the protection of easements depended on the doctrine of notice. Legal easements would bind the world. Equitable easements would bind all except the bona fide purchaser of a legal estate for value without notice.

Under the Unregistered Title system legal easements still bound the world. Equitable easements created before 1926 still depended on the doctrine of notice for their survival. Equitable easements created after 1925 are registrable as Class D(iii) Land Charges (section 2 *Land Charges Act 1972*) which should be registered in the name of the estate owner whose estate is affected. By section 4 of the *Land Charges Act 1972*, an equitable easement created after 1926 if unregistered is void against a purchaser for money or money's worth of a legal estate in the land. Exceptions have been made, however, for equitable easements arising by estoppel. See *E R Ives Investment v. High*, above in Chap. 2 on Protection of Interests in Land.

Under the Registered Ttitle system legal easements are by section 70(1)(a) overriding interests which bind a purchaser without any requirement for registration. Equitable easements should be entered as minor interests on the land certificate of the estate owner. Exceptions have been made where openly enjoyed and exercised equitable easements have been regarded as not being required to be entered upon the Register and are thus also overriding. See *Celsteel v. Alton House* and *Thatcher v. Douglas* above in Chap. 2 On Protection of Interests in Land.

Profits à Prendre

A profit is a property right related to easements. A profit is the right to take something which is part of the land or the right to take something off the land which is susceptible to ownership when taken. Examples of the former include peat, turf, wood gravel or sand. Examples of the latter include game or fish though not wild animals. For a relatively modern example of litigation on these unusual rights, see *Newman v. Bennett* [1981] Q.B. 726 where it was held that a right to take grass by grazing was not just a defence to trespass but a right of pasture over the land. In exercising that right the dominant owner had to observe local bye-laws.

10. FREEHOLD COVENANTS

Who is a Covenantee?

Generally the covenantee is the person in whose favour the covenant has been made and is usually a party to the contract or deed containing the covenant. The covenant is enforceable against the covenantor by the covenantee because there is a privity of contract between them. However, the definition of a covenantee has been extended by section 56 of the *Law of Property Act 1925* and may, in some instances, include a person who was not party to the contract or the deed.

KEY PRINCIPLE: *"A person may take an immediate or other interest in land or other property, or the benefit of any condition, right of entry, covenant or agreement over or respecting land or other property, although he may not be named as a party to the conveyance or other instrument"—Section 56 (1) of the* Law of Property Act 1925.

Re Ecclesiastical Commissioners' Conveyance 1936

In 1887, the Ecclesiastical Commissioners conveyed a freehold house and land known as "West Heath House" to H G Gotto. H G Gotto covenanted to observe a number of restrictive covenants for himself, his assigns and also all future owners and tenants of the said land. As a separate covenant, he covenanted with the assigns and owners for the time being of the lands adjoining or adjacent to the land conveyed to him that he would observe these covenants. Several other plots of land adjoining or near West Heath House which was conveyed to H G Gotto, had been conveyed to the respective purchasers prior to the conveyance of 1887 by the Ecclesiastical Commissioners. The owners of West Heath House sought a declaration that West Heath House conveyed to H G Gotto was no longer subject to the restrictive covenants or in the alternative, a determination as to which of the covenants were enforceable and by whom.

HELD: (Ch.D.) On a true construction of the covenant, the original covenantees, who were the purchasers of land which was near to or adjoining West Heath House, and the present owners of such land was entitled to enforce the covenants although the original covenantees were not parties to the conveyance of 1887. [1936] 1 Ch. 430.

White v. Bijou Mansions Ltd 1938

In 1887 the owners of a freehold estate sold part of the property to F who covenanted to build a house on it and to use it as a private residence. The vendors entered into reciprocal covenants with F that any subsequent sale or grant of a lease would contain inter alia a covenant to use the land for the purposes of private dwelling houses only. The plaintiff derived title from F.

In 1890, the same owners of the freehold estate sold adjoining land to N, who entered into covenants with the owners and their assigns similar to those with F. The land subsequently became vested in P. P granted a 28-year lease to lessees who afterwards assigned it to the defendants. The defendants sought to convert the house into a set of private suites. The plaintiff sought to restrain the defendant from breaching the covenant.

HELD: (C.A.) The covenant in 1890 was between N and the owners of the freehold estate. There was no indication from the covenant that F or the plaintiff was to benefit from the covenant and thus the plaintiff was not entitled to enforce the covenant against the defendant. [1938] Ch. 351.

COMMENTARY

In *White v. Bijou Mansions*, since the covenant made no reference to the fact that the covenant was to be for the benefit of any person other than the covenantee and his assigns, the plaintiff was not entitled to the benefit of the covenant under section 56 of the *Law of Property Act 1925*. The plaintiff's argument that his predecessor in title was the assignee of the covenantee failed. The position was different in *Re Ecclesiastical Commissioners*, where the covenant was specifically made with the owners of the land which had previously been sold. Therefore, the owners of these properties could enforce the covenant as they received the benefit of it by virtue of section 56 of the *Law of Property Act 1925*. This approach has been followed recently in *Amsprop Trading Ltd v. Harris Distribution*, *The Times*, November 13, 1996. Neuberger J. decided that in order for a third party to take the benefit of a covenant even though he was not a party to the contract, the contract must be purported to be made with him. It was enough that the third party was merely named in the contract.

Freehold Covenants at Common Law

[a] Transmission of the benefit of the covenant

KEY PRINCIPLE: *In order for the benefit of the covenant to pass to the covenantee's successors in title, the covenant must touch and concern the land.*

Smith and Snipes Hall Farm v. River Douglas Catchment Board 1949

In 1938, the defendant covenanted with the owners of some lands which were prone to flooding, adjoining Eller Brook in Lancashire, that it would replace the then defective outfall from Low Meadows situated near the junction of Eller Brook with the River Douglas, by a new outfall. It would also widen, deepen and make good the banks of the Eller Brook and maintain the work when completed for all time. This was in consideration of the land owners contributing to the costs of the works. In 1940 one of the lands was transferred, together with the benefit of the covenant, to the first plaintiff. The land was subsequent let to the second plaintiff from 1944 on a yearly tenancy. In the autumn of 1946, the brook burst its banks and flooded the plaintiffs' land. The plaintiffs claimed for damages in tort and for breach of contract.

HELD: (C.A.) That the defendant was in breach of its covenant and that such breach had resulted in the plaintiffs suffering the loss complained of. It was clear from the covenant that it affected the land as land and demonstrated an intention that benefit of the covenant was to be attached to the land. The covenant by the defendant ran with the land and by virtue of section 78 of the *Law of Property Act 1925*, it could be enforced by the covenantee and her successors in title and of persons deriving title under her or them, namely the second plaintiff and the first plaintiff. [1949] 2 K.B. 500.

COMMENTARY
Lord Justice Tucker stated in the case that the term "touches and concerns land" meant that the covenant in question must "either affect the land as regards mode of occupation, or it

must be such as per se, and not merely from collateral circumstances, affect the value of the land." On the facts of the
case, this was satisfied. It was also evident that the other
requirements for the running of the benefit of the covenant,
namely that the covenantee and her successors in title held
the same legal estate in land, and that the covenant was
intended to benefit the subsequent owners of the land, was
satisfied in this case. The covenant was therefore enforceable
by the plaintiffs against the defendant Catchment Board.

KEY PRINCIPLE: *The covenantee and his successors in title
need not have the same legal estate in the land.*

Smith and Snipes Hall Farm v. River Douglas Catchment Board 1949
(as above)

HELD: (C.A.) That the second plaintiff, who was only a tenant
of the first plaintiff, was still entitled to succeed in its claim for
damages because section 78(1) of the *Law of Property Act 1925*
had changed the common law rule requiring the covenantee
and his successors in title to have the original covenantee's
estate. [1949] 2 K.B. 500.

COMMENTARY
Section 78(1) of the *Law of Property Act 1925* deems that a
covenant is made with the covenantee, his successors in title
and with persons deriving title under him or them. This would
therefore include the second plaintiff, who was only a tenant,
and therefore did not have the same legal estate as the
covenantee, but because it derived title from the first plaintiff,
it was entitled to claim damages as a result of the section.

[b] Transmission of the burden of the covenant

KEY PRINCIPLE: *The burden of the covenant does not run
with the land at common law.*

Austerberry v. Oldham Corporation 1885
The defendants were the successor in title to a piece of land on
which a road had been built by its predecessor in title. The
predecessor in title had covenanted with the original owner
of the land, John Elliott, who was also the owner of adjoining
lands, that they would build and maintain the road. The

plaintiff was the successor in title to John Elliot's adjoining lands and sought to enforce the covenant against the defendant.

HELD: (C.A.) The plaintiff could not enforce the covenant against the defendant because the burden of a covenant imposing a positive obligation does not run with the land. (1885) 29 Ch. 750.

Rhone v. Stephens 1994

The owner of a house divided it into two dwellings in 1960. The roof of the larger dwelling ("the house") lay above the bedroom of the smaller dwelling ("the cottage"). When he sold the cottage in 1960, he covenanted for himself and his successors in title to maintain such part of the roof of the house as lies above the cottage in wind and watertight condition. In 1984, the condition of roof had detriorated and water leaked through into the bedroom of the cottage. The plaintiffs, who were successors in title to the original covenantee sought to enforce the covenant against the defendant, who was the successor in title to the original covenantor.

HELD: (H.L.) Although it was clear from the 1960 conveyance that the defendant as successor in title was the owner of the roof and was therefore in breach of the covenant to keep the roof in repair, the burden of that covenant did not run with the land at common law and the plaintiffs could not therefore enforce it against the defendant. [1994] 2 A.C. 310.

COMMENTARY

Lord Justice Tucker in *Austerberry v. Oldham Corporation* stated that ". . . I am not prepared to say that any covenant which imposes a burden upon land does run with the land, unless the covenant does, upon the true construction of the deed containing the covenant, amount to either a grant of an easement, or a rent-charge, or some estate or interest in land. A mere covenant to repair or to do something of that kind, does not seem to me, I confess, to run with the land in such a way as to bind those who may acquire it." The approach of the Court of Appeal in *Austerberry v. Oldham Corporation*, has been followed by the House of Lords in *Rhone v. Stephens*. The common law rule therefore is that the burden of a positive covenant does not run with the land at common law. The rule in *Tulk v. Moxhay* (see later) does not apply to positive covenants and therefore the burden of the covenant does not run in equity as well. There are however alternative methods of enforcing positive obligations, for example, as suggested by Tucker L.J., it could take the form of a rent charge, or an easement. It could also be through the grant of a covenant together with a chain of indemnity or a covenant imposed in a long lease instead of through a sale or through the rule in *Halsall v. Brizell* (see below).

KEY PRINCIPLE: *As an exception to the general rule that the burden of a positive covenant does not run with the land at common law, the rule in* Halsall v. Brizell *provides that a benefit cannot be taken under a deed without being subject to the obligations contained in it.*

Halsall v. Brizell 1957

The Vendors were the owners of 40 acres of land in Liverpool, which they subsequently sold off in 174 building plots. The vendors retained ownership of the roads, sewers, a promenade and sea wall. They entered into a deed with a number of the purchasers of the building plots declaring that the vendors held the roads, sewers, promenade and seawall on trust for the purchasers. The purchasers covenanted for themselves, their heirs, executors and assigns that they would contribute towards its maintenance and upkeep. The vendors covenanted on their own behalf, their heirs and assigns. In 1931, F purchased one of the plots of land together with a dwelling house built on it, which was conveyed to him subject to the covenants contained in the earlier deed. F subsequently let the property to five tenants.

Up until 1950, the owners of the various plots of land paid an equal sum per plot which was sufficient for the upkeep of the roads, sewers, promenade and sea wall. This was paid by F and upon his death by his executors. In 1950, the owners of the other plots of land agreed that additional sums would be payable where the dwelling house on any of the plots of land had been divided into two or more flats or dwellings. F's executors refused to pay this additional amount.

HELD: (Ch.D.) [a] That prima facie, the covenant contained in the deed were unenforceable, *inter alia*, because the burden of a positive covenant did not run with the land.

[b] The defendants were not entitled to take advantage of the use of the roads, and sewers contained in the original deed without being subject to the obligations contained in it. On that principle, the defendants were bound to pay the additional sums demanded.[1957] 1 Ch. 169.

COMMENTARY
The rule of mutual benefit and burden is seen as an exception to the principle that the burden of a positive covenant does not run with the land at common law. This is however restricted to the situation where the person subject to the burden also receives some benefit from the covenant otherwise it does not apply.

Freehold Covenants in Equity

[a] The characteristics of enforceable covenants in equity

KEY PRINCIPLE: *The covenantee must possess some land which can benefit from the covenant at the time the covenant is granted.*

London County Council v. Allen 1914
M J Allen covenanted with the plaintiffs that he would not build on a plot of land which lay across the end of a street proposed to be laid out by him. He covenanted for himself, his heirs and assigns, and other persons claiming under him, so far as practicable to bind the land into whosoever hands the same might come. The plaintiffs did not own any neighbouring land for the benefit of which this covenant was imposed. M J Allen subsequently sold the land to the defendant who had notice of the covenant but proceeded to build on the land without the plaintiff's consent.

HELD: (C.A.) The plaintiffs were not entitled to enforce the covenant against the defendant as it did not own any relevant land capable of benefitting from the covenant. [1914] 3 K.B. 642.

COMMENTARY
The reversion of a landlord qualifies as relevant land for this purpose—see the case of *Hall v. Ewin* (1887) 37 Ch. 74.

Transmission of the Benefit of the Covenant in Equity

Apart from satisfying the general requirments for the transmission of the benefit of the covenant, in order for the benefit of the covenant to run with the land in equity, it must be annexed to the land, assigned with the land or subject to a building scheme.

[a] Annexation

[I] Express annexation

KEY PRINCIPLE: *The benefit of the covenant is expressly annexed to the land when the words of the covenant shows that it is for the benefit of the covenantee's land.*

Rogers v. Hosegood 1900

A plot of land was conveyed by the owners to the then Duke of Bedford in 1869. The Duke covenanted that no more than one messuage or dwelling house should at any one time be erected or standing on the plot and that it would only be adapted for and used as a private residence only. It was stated that the covenant was entered into with the intent that it might so far as possible bind the premises thereby conveyed and every part thereof, into whosoever hands the same might come, and might enure to the benefit of the vendors, their heirs and assigns and others claiming under them to all or any of their lands adjoining or near the premises. The vendors who were owners of other plots of land, subsequently conveyed another plot of land near to the Duke of Bedford's land to a purchaser who had no knowledge of the earlier covenant.

The Duke of Bedford's successor in title to the plot of land proposed to build a block of residential flats on the land. The successors in title of the other plot of land sought to enforce the covenant.

HELD: (C.A.) The successors in title of the other plot of land could enforce the covenant against the successors in title of the Duke's land. The wording in the covenant showed an intention that the covenant was to run with the land and therefore was enforceable by the successors in title of the covenantee. The lack of knowledge on the part of the purchaser of the other plot of land that it had the benefit of the covenant did not prevent him or his successors in title from enforcing the covenant, provided that the benefit of the covenant had been annexed to the land. [1900] 2 Ch. 388.

Renals v. Cowlishaw 1878

Land adjoining a residential estate was sold to the defendant's predecessors in title in 1845. The latter entered into covenants with the vendors and their assigns which restricted their right to build on or use the land. The vendors subsequently sold the residential estate to the plaintiff's predecessors in title. This conveyance did not contain any reference to the restrictive covenants nor was there any representation or term in the contract that the purchasers of the residential estate would have the benefit of the covenants contained in the earlier conveyance. The plaintiff's conveyance contained a covenant limiting their use of the residential estate. The plaintiffs commenced an action to restrain the defendants from building on the adjoining land in contravention of the covenants.

HELD: (Ch.D.) Although the plaintiffs were the assigns of the covenantee, they were not entitled to sue upon the original covenants as the covenant failed to identify the land to be benefited by the covenant.(1878) 9 Ch. 125.

COMMENTARY

The difference between the two cases is that in *Rogers v. Hosegood*, the plaintiff could enforce the covenant in question as it had been expressly annexed to the land. Therefore the fact that he was ignorant of its existence was irrelevant. In *Renals v. Cowlishaw*, the covenant was not expressly annexed to the land as it had failed to identify the land which was to benefit from the covenant. As such although the plaintiffs were the assigns of the covenantee, the covenant was unenforceable.

KEY PRINCIPLE: *Where the deed creating the covenant annexes the benefit of the covenant to the whole of the land, the annexation would be ineffective unless it is clear that the covenant confers an actual benefit on the whole of the land and not merely part thereof.*

Re Ballard's Conveyance 1937

The applicant was the purchaser of 18 acres of a 1,700 acre estate. He covenanted with the vendor, her heirs and assigns and successors in title on behalf of himself, his heirs and assigns-that they would be bound by the covenants contained in a schedule to the conveyance. The applicant applied for a declaration under section 84 of the *Law of Property Act 1925* that his property was no longer affected by the covenants contained in the earlier conveyance.

HELD: (Ch.D.) Where a restrictive covenant purports to be annexed to the land but does not in fact concern and touch the whole of the land (but merely part of it), the annexation is ineffective and the covenant does not run with the land and cannot be enforced by any owner of the land except the covenantee. [1937] Ch. 473.

COMMENTARY

(1) Clauson J. stated that ". . . It appears to me quite obvious that while a breach of the stipulations might possibly affect a portion of that area in the vicinity of the applicant's land, far the largest part of this area of 1700 acres could not possibly be affected by any breach of the stipulations." The conclusion was that as the covenants were not such as could benefit the whole of the land, the covenants could not be enforced by subsequent owners of the land. However, where it is made clear in the stipulation that the covenant benefits whole or any part or parts of the retained land, then the covenant is valid and effective: *Marquess of Zetland v. Driver* [1939]1 Ch. 1.

(2) The strict approach in *Re Ballard's Conveyance* has not always been followed. In *Wrotham Park Estate Co Ltd v. Parkside Homes Ltd* [1974] 1 W.L.R. 798, the court took the view that a convenant could benefit the whole of a 4,000-acre estate spread over three sites where the owners were satisfied that the covenant could be regarded as benefiting the whole of the land which it was intended to protect.

[ii] Statutory annexation

KEY PRINCIPLE: *The benefit of the covenant can be annexed to the land by the operation of section 78 of the* Law of Property Act 1925.

Federated Homes Ltd v. Mill Lodge Properties Ltd 1980

M owned three plots of land which were described as the blue land, the red land and the green land. M sold the blue land to the defendant who agreed not to build more than 300 dwellings on it ("the covenant"). The other two plots of land was subsequently sold by M. The plaintiff later became the owner of both these two plots of land but had acquired it from different vendors. The benefit of the covenant was passed to the plaintiff as owner of the green land through an unbroken chain of assignments from the original covenantee. The defendant decided to build in contravention of the covenant not to build more than 300 dwellings on the land. The plaintiff sought to prevent this. The covenant was therefore enforceable against the defendant by the plaintiff as owner of the green land. The plaintiff further argued that the covenant was enforceable against the defendant, as owner of the red land. It argued that section 62 or 78 of the *Law of Property Act 1925* allowed it to do so as the covenant "touched and concerned" the land.

HELD: (C.A.) As the covenant touched and concerned the land belonging to the covenantee, the benefit of the covenant was therefore annexed to the land under section 78 of the *Law of Property Act 1925*. The covenant was enforceable against the defendant. [1980] 1 All E.R. 371.

COMMENTARY

Brightman L.J. stated that ". . . if the precondition precedent to section 78 is satisfied—that is to say, there exists a covenant which touches and concerns the land of the covenantee—that covenant runs with the land for the benefit of his successors in title, persons deriving title under him or them and other owners and occupiers." Therefore, it would appear that so long as the covenant is one which touches and concerns the land, the benefit of that covenant is one which is annexed to the land under section 78 of the *Law of Property Act 1925*. The successors in title to the covenantee or persons deriving title under him or them can enforce the covenant against the covenantor or his successors in title or persons deriving title under him or them. This has been subject to much academic criticism. See for example Preston and Newsom, *Restrictive Covenants Affecting Freehold Land* (7th edn).

KEY PRINCIPLE: *Section 78 of the Law of Property Act 1925 can be excluded by a contrary intention.*

Roake v. Chadha 1983

A house was sold in 1834 subject to a covenant that no more than one private dwelling house would be built on the land. The deed stipulated that the covenant would not enure for the benefit of any owner or subsequent purchaser of the covenantee's land unless the benefit of the covenant was expressly assigned. The plaintiffs were the successors in title to the covenantee's land and the defendant was the successor in title to the covenantor's land. The defendant proposed to build an additional house on the land. The plaintiffs sought a declaration that they were entitled to the benefit of the covenant and an injunction to restrain the defendant from erecting another house on the land.

HELD: (Ch.D.) The plaintiffs were not entitled to the benefit of the covenant. Although section 78 of the *Law of Property Act 1925* did not allow for its provisions to be excluded by contrary agreement, the covenant had to be construed as a whole to see if the benefit of the covenant was annexed to the land. Where the covenant was not qualified in any way, annexation could be readily inferred. However, as the covenant expressly stipulated that the benefit of the covenant could only enure for the benefit of any owner or subsequent purchaser by express assignment, the benefit of the covenant could not be said to have been annexed to the land. [1983] 3 All E.R. 503.

COMMENTARY
The effect of this decision is that section 78 of the *Law of Property Act 1925* can be excluded by a contrary intention. This is notwithstanding that section 78 is silent on this issue in comparison with section 79 of the same Act which expressly allows for the latter to be excluded.

[iii] Implied annexation

KEY PRINCIPLE: *In the absence of express annexation and notwithstanding that the land to be benefitted by the covenant is not identified in the covenant, the identity of the land could be implied from the circumstances of the case.*

Marten v. Flight Refuelling Ltd 1962

In 1942, the Air Ministry requisitioned 200 acres of a farm of 562 acres which was part of a large agricultural estate. The farm was conveyed in 1943 to the sitting tenant who, *inter alia*, covenanted with the vendors and their successors in title that no part of the land or any building on it would be used for any purposes other than agricultural purposes without the written consent of the vendors or their agents. The covenant was registered as a Class D (ii) land charge in 1943. In 1947 the Air Ministry let a commercial company into occupation giving rights over the aerodrome. The nature of the company's business included maintainance of the airfield and its facilities, design and development of air refuelling equipment and other miscellaneous industrial and commercial activities. In 1958, the Air Ministry compulsorily purchased a large part of the requisitioned land subject to the covenant. It also subsequently purchased the remaining part of the requisitioned land free of the restriction.

An action was commenced against the Air Ministry by the plaintiffs alleging breach of covenant by the Air Ministry.

HELD: (Ch.D.) That having regard to the circumstances surrounding the 1943 conveyance, and taking a broad and reasonable view of the proof an identity of the estate, it could be shown with reasonable certainty that the covenant was taken for the benefit of land belonging to the vendor. Therefore, it did not matter that the covenant did not expressly annex or identify the land to be benefited. As the plaintiffs together represented the whole legal and equitable interest in the covenant, they were therefore entitled to a declaration that they were entitled to the benefit of the covenant. [1962] 1 Ch. 117.

Newton Abbot Co-operative Society v. Williamson and Treadgold Ltd 1952

The covenantee was the owner of a property known as Devonia in Bovey Tracey where she carried on the business of an ironmonger. The original covenantor was the purchaser of a property belonging to the covenantee opposite Devonia. The conveyance contained a covenant by the purchaser not to carry on the business of an ironmonger on the property. No reference was made as to the land which was to benefit from this covenant. The business of the covenantee was subsequently assigned by her son, together with the benefit of the covenant to a co-operative society. The co-operative society subsequently amalgamated with the plaintiff society. The plaintiffs commenced an action against the assigns of the covenantor to enforce the covenant.

HELD: (Ch.D.) There was nothing in the conveyance which identified the land for the benefit of which the covenant was taken. However, the court was entitled to look at the attendant circumstances to see if the land to benefitted was shown otherwise with reasonable certainty. The plaintiffs were entitled to an injunction enabling them to enforce the restrictive covenant. [1952]1 Ch. 286.

COMMENTARY
Although *Newton Abbot Co-operative Society v. Williamson and Treadgold Ltd* suggested that the land to be benefited could be inferred from the circumstances, it was merely an *obiter dicta*. The case was decided on the basis of the assignment of the benefit of the covenant (see later). It would therefore appear that *Marten v. Flight Refuelling Ltd*, is the only case where the court was prepared to hold that there could be an implied annexation of the benefit of the covenant. See also *J Sainsbury plc v. Enfield London Borough Council* [1989] 1 W.L.R. 590.

[b] Assignment

KEY PRINCIPLE: *The successor in title to the original covenantee's land can enforce a restrictive covenant if he or she can demonstrate that the benefit of the covenant has been assigned to him or her.*

Newton Abbot Co-operative Society v. Williamson and Treadgold Ltd 1952
(see above)

HELD: (Ch.D.) That as the covenantee's son had the benefit of the covenant in equity he was entitled to assign it to the co-operative society. The assigns of the covenantee was therefore entitled to enforce the covenant against the defendants.

COMMENTARY
The assignees of the benefit of the covenant can enforce a covenant against the covenantor or his assignees. However,

in order to do so, it is necessary for the former to be able to
establish an unbroken chain of assignments from the original
covenantee to the current owner of the land to be benefitted
from the covenant. If the chain of assignment is broken, then
the covenant is not enforceable unless it can be shown that
the benefit of the covenant has been either annexed to the
land or it forms part of a scheme of development.

[c] Building schemes

KEY PRINCIPLE: *Where the requirements of a building
scheme are satisfied, the owners of the respective lots of
land in such a scheme have the benefit of mutually enforceable covenants.*

Elliston v. Reacher 1908

In 1860, a Building Society acquired the title to an estate in
Felixstowe. Part of the estate had been laid out in plots and was
shown in the sale plans of the society. The plan contained
conditions which were to affect the different plots of land.
The conditions stipulated that each purchaser was to execute
a deed of covenant for regulating building on the respective
plots and securing performance of the covenants contained in it
which included a covenant that no hotel should be built on any
lot and no building should be used as asas a hotel without the
vendors' consent. Three of the plots of land was sold to plaintiffs' predecessors in title and another two plots were sold to the
defendants' predecessors in title. The plaintiffs commenced an
action against the defendants to restrain them from using a
building as a hotel in breach of the covenant.

HELD: (Ch.D.) That the covenant was enforceable against the
defendants and therefore could be restrained by injunction.
[1908] 2 Ch. 374.

COMMENTARY
(1) The decision of Parker J. was affirmed on appeal by the
Court of Appeal (reported at [1908] 2 Ch. 665). The importance of Parker J.'s decision is with respect to the conditions
which is to be satisfied in order for a building scheme to be
established, resulting in covenants being mutually enforceable by the owners of the respective plots of land in the
scheme.

(2) He stated (at p. 384) that ". . . it must be proved (1) that both the plaintiffs and defendants derive title under a common vendor; (2) that previously to selling the lands to which the plaintiffs and defendants are respectively entitled the vendor laid out his estate, or a defined portion thereof (including the lands purchased by the plaintiffs and defendants respectively), for sale in lots subject to restrictions intended to be imposed on all the lots, and which, though varying in details as to particular lots, are consistent and consistent only with some general scheme of development; (3) that these restrictions were intended by the common vendor to be and were for the benefit of all the lots intended to be sold, whether or not they were also intended to be and were for the benefit of other land retained by the vendor; and (4) that both the plaintiffs and the defendants, or their predecessors in title, purchased their lots from the common vendor upon the footing that the restrictions subject to which the purchases were made were to enure for the benefit of the other lots included in the general scheme whether or not they were also to enure for the benefit of other lands retained by the vendors."

KEY PRINCIPLE: *A scheme of development can be found to have been established even though the scheme may lack a common vendor and the land was not laid out in plots.*

Baxter v. Four Oaks Properties Ltd 1965

C, the owner of a large estate conveyed part of it to H in 1891 and by an indenture made at the same time between C, H and all other persons who might subsequently purchase any part of the estate, it was agreed that H and all the other purchasers, their heirs, assigns and persons claiming under them should observe and perform the covenants and conditions set out in the schedule. It was further provided that the covenants and conditions were enforceable by any other person entitled for the time being of any other land forming part of the estate. There was no evidence that C had laid out the estate in lots prior to any sale taking place and C sold the lots in accordance with the purchaser's requirements. The plaintiffs and defendant were the successors in title to the original purchasers from C. The plaintiffs sought to enforce a restrictive covenant against the defendant.

HELD: (Ch.D.) Where it is clear that the intention of the parties was that the various purchasers from a common vendor of parts of an estate should have rights as against each other, the court would given effect to that intention notwithstanding that the vendor had not laid out the estate in lots prior to the commencement of sales. [1965] Ch. 816.

Re Dolphin's Conveyance 1970

In 1871, two sisters who were the owners of a 30-acre estate, sold four plots of land to four different purchasers with a covenant that they would build only detached houses of plots of no less than a quarter acre. The purchasers further covenanted that they would obtain similar covenants from subsequent purchasers of any part of the estate. One of the sisters died in 1873. The estate subsequently passed to their nephew who sold off the remaining estate in six parcels, obtaining similar covenants from the purchasers with the exception of thelastthe last parcel of land. The plaintiffs acquired part of the estate with notice of the covenants and wished to build dwelling houses in contravention of covenant. The plaintiffs applied for a declaration *inter alia*, that their land was no longer subject to or affected by the restrictive covenants, arguing that there was no building scheme.

HELD: (Ch.D.) The plaintiffs' land was subject to the restrictive covenants. A building scheme existed where on the true construction of the various conveyances, it is clear that the covenants were imposed for the common benefit of all the purchasers and vendors of the estate. It was evident that the covenants were to be enforceable between the purchasers against each other and all of them had a common interest in such enforcement. [1970] Ch. 654.

COMMENTARY

(1) In *Re Dolphin's Conveyance*, Stamp J. was prepared to hold that a building scheme existed on the basis that it was clearly intended by all the parties concerned that a local law be laid down for the estate for the benefit of all the separate purchasers. He did so in reliance of the principle laid down in the earlier case of *Baxter v. Four Oaks Properties Ltd* that the existence or evidence of mutual obligation and reciprocity were the main characteristics of a building scheme.

(2) Whether or not a building scheme is intended is a question of fact in each case. In the recent Privy Council decision of *Emile Elias & Co Ltd v. Pine Grove Ltd* [1993] 1 W.L.R. 305, the Privy Council was of the view that on the facts of that case no building scheme was intended. This was because as all the lots were all of a similar nature and were all intended for a high class development, a disparity of the covenants imposed was a clear indication that there was no intention to create reciprocally enforceable rights.

Discharge and Modification of Covenants

KEY PRINCIPLE: *Under section 84 of the* Law of Property Act 1925, *the Lands Tribunal has the power to modify or discharge any restrictive covenant in accordance with the criteria set out in that section.*

Re Beech's Application 1990

The owner of a council house applied for the discharge of a restrictive covenant restricting the use of the house as a private dwelling, so as to enable him to convert it into office accommodation.

HELD: (Lands Tribunal) The restriction would not be discharged as it would have an adverse impact on the area.

COMMENTARY
The case is merely an example as to how the Lands Tribunal exercises its power under section 84 of the *Law of Property Act 1925*. Other recent examples on the application of section 84 can be seen in cases such as *Re Love and Love's Application* (1993) 67 P. & C.R. 101 and *National Schizophrenia Fellowship v. Ribble Estates* S.A. (1993) 25 H.L.R. 476.

INDEX